Imprint On The Nation

Stories Reflecting The National Guard's Impact on a Changing Nation

by
Martin K. Gordon

ISBN 0-89745-039-6

Sunflower University Press
1531 YUMA (BOX 1009) • MANHATTAN, KANSAS 66502, USA

University of Charleston Library
Charleston, WV 25304

355.37
G657;

Foreword, Table of Contents,
and all bibliographies are copyright 1983
by
Martin K. Gordon

This book is one of a first printing
of 1500 copies.

Preface

These short essays reflect the many areas in which the nation's militiamen — Guardsmen in the twentieth century — have made an imprint on not only the military history of the United States, but also on its culture. The National Guard has always been part of the basic fabric of American life. I have tried through these essays to show something of the variety of avenues through which "The Guard" has become integrated into our culture. Be the event war, disaster, or a peaceful commemoration of one of our national festivals, the citizen-soldiers of the states are always there. It is that presence that most intrigued me about the National Guard as I wrote these articles.

This series of vignettes of military history began in January 1976 and ran monthly for four years. The National Guard Bureau published them in its newsletter, *Push Pin Post*. A note at the bottom of the bibliography which accompanies each essay identifies the issue of the newsletter in which it appeared. Several military and private magazines have reprinted a few of these essays, but they have not been collected in one publication before this book. Except for the essay (#16) never published before, their first appearance was always in *Push Pin Post*.

I compiled the bibliographies for this publication. They are a record of the principal sources I used, and not definitive lists of publications and sources for each subject. I have indicated in each bibliography where I have added items published after my essay or items published earlier that I thought the reader should know about.

I would particularly like to acknowledge the assistance of the staff of the Organizational History Branch of the United States Army Center of Military History. Especially, Miss Janice E. McKenney, the Branch Chief Mr. John B. Wilson, and Dr. Robert K. Wright, Jr. Their files are repeatedly cited in the bibliographies. I must, however, accept full responsibility for any mistakes in this book. Likewise, the opinions expressed herein are mine, and do not necessarily reflect the views or policies of any Federal agency.

Martin K. Gordon
Columbia, Maryland
September 1982

Foreword

In all of the attention which has been paid to U.S. military history it has often struck me as ironic that there is such a dearth of literature on the oldest of our nation's military institutions, the National Guard.

The National Guard is, in accordance with the provisions of the Dick Act of 1903, the proper successor to the organized militia which traces its ancestry to the earliest of colonial times.

This collection of essays by Martin K. Gordon promises to go a long way toward the correction of the deficiency noted above. This collection is a vivid demonstration of the widespread and yet localized character of the Guard. In its panoply of parades, its great urban armories, its responses to disaster, its historic places and its colorful people, Gordon has succeeded in showing something of the face of the soldiers of the States and their long tradition of setting aside civilian world responsibilities to participate in the nation's wars and battles.

An important historical aspect to this work is its reaffirmation of the continuity which enables many of today's National Guard units to be identified with the colorful militia antecedents of yesteryear. As seen through Martin Gordon's eyes, the National Guard is indeed a representation of the *types* of communities and the reasons why they were prompted to provide military organizations for the State and for the Nation. The overall effect is to create an identity for the National Guard as a peculiarly American institution, a reflection of the American ethos and one which remained relatively constant as the nation pushed westward from the Atlantic seaboard and as the rural land gave way to the great wave of industrialization and urbanization. The Guard would evolve as a solid institution just as meaningful and essential to Chicago as to Norwich.

A creation of the framers of the Constitution in many ways, the Guard (or Militia) was initially viewed as being needed to help enforce the laws of the land, to repel invasion or to supress insurrection. It was left pretty much to its own (or, rather, the States' own) devices from the passage of the Militia Act of 1792 to 1903 when the Dick Act heralded the dawn of a new era and the start of the emergence of the Guard as a "dual status" force with both State and Federal missions.

During 1903-16, while the issue of dual status was being argued in the Congress, in the War Department and even in the White House, the Guard embarked upon a series of evolutionary moves which marked — albeit to the regret of old diehards — the start of the transition away from ceremonial functions to full dedication to field service.

More important than the change in the hue of uniforms was the conformity of National Guard organization structure with that of the Regular Army. The State troops which were mustered for service on the Mexican Border in 1916 were hammered and moulded into the Army which became the American Expeditionary Force on the battlefields of France in 1918.

The National Guard which came out of this experience with its head high (after all, the German High Command had noted that three of the best five divisions in the AEF were National Guard divisions) was destined from that time forward to march down the road which leads to the important role which it plays today in the Total Force Policy. It is a simple fact of life that the elements of the National Guard today are an essential ingredient of this nation's military strategy.

Thus the role of the National Guard as we near the end of the 20th century and have recently passed the second century of the nation's independence is a triumph for those who engineered and believed in the dual status concept of the National Guard. It has worked well, and Martin Gordon's collection of essays create an interesting mosaic which illustrates the many facets of "the Guard."

Bruce Jacobs
Major General, Army National Guard
Publisher
National Guard Magazine

Acknowledgements

First, a special acknowledgment to Ms. Hazel M. Humphries, Chief, Documentation and History, Office of Public Affairs, National Guard Bureau, not only for encouraging and supporting this series as it was first developed, but also for permission to collect and reprint the essays and National Guard artwork that accompanies several of them. Following the order in which the illustrations appear in the text, I here thank these individuals and institutions for permission to use illustrations from their collections: Mrs. Gay Neufeld Santelli; National Guard Association of the United States; Worcester Art Museum; Metropolitan Museum of Art; Henry Francis du Pont Winterthur Museum; New York Historical Society; Martin Luther King, Jr., Memorial Library of Washington, DC; Milwaukee County Historical Society; Mr. W. S. Jones, Historian of the Chatham Artillery of Savannah, Georgia; Stackpole Books; Richmond Newspapers, Inc.; Enoch Pratt Free Library of Baltimore, Maryland; Yale University Library; Bedford, Massachusetts Free Public Library; Oregon State Department of Transportation; Chicago Historical Society; Mr. Irving L. London, formerly of the Camera Shop of Johnstown, Pennsylvania; and, the Bancroft Library of the University of California. The curators and archivists of the National Park Service, The Library of Congress, and the National Archives helped me locate many useful illustrations, all of which are in the public domain. I also used several illustrations from John Grafton, *The American Revolution: A Picture Sourcebook* (New York: Dover Publications, Inc., 1975).

Table of Contents

Preface ii
Foreword iii
Acknowledgements iv

No.	Subject	Page

Participation In America's Wars Colonial Warfare
1. "... And Not Only Indians" 1
   See Also: Anniversaries: "1736: The Guard's One Hundredth Year"

The American Revolution
2. "Marksmanship: An Early Report" 3
3. "Militiamen Save West Point" 5
4. "Citizen Soldier to Continental Regular: Glover's Marblehead Mariners" 7
   See Also: The Ethnic Heritage of the Guard: "The Black Militia and the Revolution"

The Civil War
5. "Those Devils in Baggy Pants" 9
   See Also: Anniversaries: "The Soldiers of August: The Civil War"
   The Ethnic Heritage of the Guard: "Prelude to Bravery," "The New Mexico Militia in the Civil War"

World War II
6. "I Bowed Briefly on the Grim Corregidor" 11
7. "Operation Bob Cat: The National Guard on Bora Bora" 13
   See Also: Soldiers of the States: "What Do You Do When the Guard is Away"

The Air Guard
8. "Nebraska Takes to the Skies" 15
9. "Much Better Late Than Never: ANGR 210.3" 17
   See Also: Personalities: "Charles A. Lindbergh: Guardsman"

Anniversaries and Turning Points
10. "1736: The Guard's One Hundredth Year" 19

11. "1836: The Guard's Two Hundredth Year" 21
12. "The Soldiers of August: Part I, 1675-1777" 23
13. "The Soldiers of August: Part II, 1779-1824" 25
14. "The Soldiers of August: The Civil War" 27
15. "The Soldiers of August: The Transition to Today's Guard" 29
16. "300 Years of the National Guard: In Celebration of the 200th Anniversary of the United States" 31

The Cultural Life of the Guard
17. "Preaching at the Militia" 35
18. "John Philip Sousa: Martial Music for the Militia" 37

The Ethnic Heritage of the Guard: The Black Militia
19. "The Black Militia and the Revolution" 39
20. "The Battalion of Free Men of Color" 41
21. "A Prelude to Bravery" 43
22. "Black History Month: A Time for Remembering" 45

The Hispanic Militia
23. "The Milicias Disciplindas de Puerto Rico" 47
24. "The New Mexico Militia in the Civil War" 49

More Ethnic Groups
25. "Jews, Discrimination, and the Militia" 51
26. "The Ethnic Militia of Early Milwaukee" 53

No.	Subject	Page

Historic Continuities

27 "On Being Alert" 55
28 "The Oldest of Them All: The Massachusetts 101st Engineer Battalion and 182nd Infantry" 57
29 "The Chatham Artillery: A Holiday Toast" 59
30 "The Saga of the Norwich Light Infantry: Only You Can Save Your History" 61
31 "The Richmond Light Infantry Blues" 63
32 " 'Remember the Alamo' — Motto of the 141st Infantry" 65
33 "Pennsylvania's 28th Infantry Division: The Bloody Bucket" 67

Personalities, Presidents and the Guard

34 "Thomas Jefferson and the Militia" 69
35 "Edgar Allan Poe: Pot, Author, and Sometime Militiaman" 71
36 "The President Had Been in the Militia" 73
37 "Charles A. Lindbergh: Guardsman" 75

The Physical Presence of the Guard

38 "The Bedford Flag" 77
39 "The Militia Flag That Helped Catch an Assassin" 79
40 "It's Your History Too" 81
41 "Your Summer Vacation: Part I" 83
42 "Your Summer Vacation: Part II" 85

Soldiers on State Missions

43 "The Great Chicago Fire" 87
44 "The Johnstown Flood" 89
45 "Yes, the Guard Helped, but . . ." 91
46 "The Hatfields, The McCoys, and the Citizen-Soldiers Get Involved in a Famous Feud" 93
47 "What Do You Do When the Guard is Away?" 95

Technology

48 "New Technology Nineteenth Century Style: The Bicycle as a Military Weapon" 97

"... AND NOT ONLY INDIANS"

The military experience of the first settlers to reach the New World was limited to frontier defense against the Indians for the first 80 years of our history, 1607-1689. While European was fighting European or Turk, the English, Spanish, and French settlers all escaped both those conflicts and the development it implied for professional soldiers.

The Indians posed very serious dangers to the colonists until after the American Revolution. Towards the end of the period the South Carolinians, for example, had to arm a force of blacks to help 600 white men defeat the Yamassee Indians in the war of 1715. But the growth in warfare between the major powers in the New World changed the usual pattern of militia and Indian allies combining to defeat other Indians. Just as the Carolinas and later Georgia were to bear the brunt of wars with Spain in the 1700s, the New England colonies, and later Virginia, were in the equivalent of the front lines in combat against France.

The change towards fighting in European-caused conflicts and with British regulars against French or Spanish regulars and militia began with King William's War, 1689-1697, the first of four French and Indian wars. On 8 February 1690 a party of Canadians and Indians attacked Schenectady, New York, changing their target from the well-defended city of Albany. Inexplicably, Schenectady's gates were guarded only by two snow men that night! The raiders killed 60 inhabitants and carried off 27 more. Both black and white residents suffered from this carelessness. A force of Albany militia and friendly Mohawk Indians pursued but were unable to stop the fleeing enemy. The war continued. Massachusetts militiamen captured Port Royal, Nova Scotia on 19 May of the same year.

The pattern of warfare that was to last throughout the 1700s now began to evolve. Regulars and militia, supported by friendly Indians, would fight a similarly composed force on the other side. Those early raids also presaged a new trend in the American militia that was to be developed throughout the century. While all able-bodied colonials still defended their homes and colonies, volunteers came to be used increasingly for those relatively long-ranged and long-lasting conflicts.

Queen Anne's War, 1702-1713, also

Fort Frederica built by General James Oglethorpe in 1736 for protection of English settlements in Georgia against Spanish advances. A center of militia activities in that era. (Photo courtesy of Miss Gay M. Neufeld)

known as the War of the Spanish Succession, brought combat to both northern and southern colonies. In the south, October 1702, Governor James Moore of South Carolina gathered some 500 militia and 300 Indians to take Fort San Marcos at St. Augustine, Florida, before the French could reinforce the Spanish garrison there. The moated stone fort of the Spanish withstood the siege. When Spanish warships appeared before the cannon Moore requested from Jamaica could arrive, he retreated. Deerfield, Massachusetts was sacked in February 1704. Later Pensacola, Florida was attacked twice in retaliation for an attack on Charleston, South Carolina by the Spanish. Montreal and Quebec were also unsuccessfully assaulted. It was in these wars that the settlers of the thirteen British North American colonies found that they could stand up to the regular forces of Europe with or without the help of the British Army.

Thirty years of peace varied with border raids and sporadic battles lasted to the beginning of the next war in 1744, King George's War. The activities of the Georgia militia exemplified the military actions carried out in those challenging years of war and peace. In 1736, Governor James Oglethorpe built Fort Frederica on St. Simon's Island, followed by the construction of some lesser forts. The Spanish protested. England, in a trading dispute, declared war on Spain in 1739. As soon as word of the war reached Oglethorpe, he raided Spanish Florida. The following year with a combination of militia, regulars, and Indians, he laid siege to St. Augustine. After ships from Cuba resupplied the fort, Oglethorpe raised the siege and returned home. In May 1742, a Spanish force of Cubans, Florida militia, and Spanish regulars, which included a black regiment, assaulted Fort Frederica in turn. Oglethorpe inflicted time-gaining defeats on the Spanish in the field and a relief squadron arrived from Charleston in time to cause the Spanish to retreat. The war in the south went on for another two years.

In the north, a joint force of New England militia and British naval ships captured the French fortress of Louisbourg, which guarded the St. Lawrence River. The war ended and the French and Indian War of 1755-1762 came. The English colonial militia practiced their skills against French regulars, militia, and Indians. The British regulars serving with those militia formed a low opinion of their informal organizations and discipline. However, George Washington, Virginia militia, and many others were gaining valuable combat experience.

When the War for American Independence came, the colonial militia were experienced in European as well as frontier warfare because they had fought and defeated the regulars of France and Spain and not only Indians.

—MARTIN K. GORDON

"...AND NOT ONLY INDIANS"

BIBLIOGRAPHY

McMaster, Fitzhugh. <u>Soldiers and Uniforms: South Carolina Military Affairs, 1670-1775</u>. Tricentennial Booklet No. 10. Columbia, SC: Published for the South Carolina Tricentennial Commission by the University of South Carolina Press, 1971.

Peckham, Howard H. <u>The Colonial Wars, 1689-1762</u>. The Chicago History of American Civilization Series. Chicago: Univ. of Chicago Press, 1964.

Shy, John. <u>A People Numerous and Armed: Reflections on the Military Struggle for Independence</u>. New York: Oxford Univ. Press, 1976.

This essay orginally appeared in the May 1977 <u>Push Pin Post</u>

Marksmanship: an early report

Marksmanship hasn't always been considered as important as it is in today's National Guard. There have been times when the soldier on the battlefield has been forced to substitute courage and quick thinking for the skills that better peacetime practice would have given him. Of course at the time of the American Revolution, when the British Army didn't even have a command for aiming the musket, the weapons didn't permit of training such as today's skill Qualification Tests (SQTs). At the series of skirmishes and battles known as Lexington and Concord in April 1775, the most common musket in use by both sides, the brown Bess, had a range of less than 125 yards and probably had an untrue bore. The British infantry frequently used their muskets, with their 21-inch bayonets, as spears in its bayonet charges. The American rebels, not as well equipped with bayonets, used their muskets as clubs in close-in fighting. Training in this context means learning how to load and fire one's firearm quickly and smoothly while under fire. The organized militia away from the frontier rarely had that training because of infrequent drill days, perhaps as few as four per year, and the scarcity and expense of gunpowder.

Origin of the minuteman.

As tensions built in 1775, Massachusetts continued the reorganization of her militia. The concept of the minutemen began to spread throughout the province. Under that concept, the officers of each company, already screened for their loyalty to the new authorities, selected a third of their companies to be ready to act "at a minute's notice." At the other end of the organizational scale, "alarm companies" were also organized. They were the last reserve of the organized militia, being composed of boys, old men, and males otherwise exempt from the militia draft. All three, minutemen, standard militia units, and alarm companies fought along with angry individual volunteers in the combat of April 19, 1775.

That was the day the British sent a strong raiding party from Boston to seize the rebel military supplies at Concord. The night of the 18th, as the British infantry prepared to march the next morning, Paul Revere, William Dawes, and others alerted the patriot forces. The militia began to gather and march towards Concord. Some of them did not arrive until the British were already in retreat. Approximately 70 Lexington militia mustered at Lexington Green to oppose some six to eight hundred elite soldiers. The British ordered the Americans to disperse and to lay down their weapons. The Americans, seeing the hopelessness of resistence at that time, agreed to disperse but not to turn their weapons over to the invaders. Then someone, unknown to this day, fired a shot. That began not only the sporadic combat of the day but also the military role in the American Revolution. The British continued to Concord, seized some supplies, and began to retreat back to the Boston area.

Many shots, few hits

Each militia or minuteman was supposed to carry 36 cartridges or its equivalent in loose powder and bullets. In that day of running skirmishes and continually arriving reinforcements, most

The American Revolution (Dover Pictorial Archives Series) The British retreat from Concord while under fire from the American militia.

militiamen would leave once they had expended their ammunition and someone arrived to take their place. Thus, although probably a total of 3,763 militia were involved in the day's fighting, perhaps not more than half were on the field against the initial detachment and its reinforcements at any one time. The British force peaked at approximately 1800.

Historian Christopher Ward has calculated from those figures, that even if each rebel present had only fired 20 shots, a total of more than 75,000 shots would have been fired at the British that day. Furthermore, if each American had hit a British soldier only once, the invaders would have been completely destroyed. Estimates of British casualties that day are 73 killed, 174 to 193 wounded, and 22 to 26 missing or captured. That totals slightly less than 300. That can be translated into one bullet out of every 250 to 300 hitting its target. (That figure is not out of line with ammunition consumption estimates for more recent wars.) The Americans lost an estimated 49 killed, 39 to 41 wounded, and five missing.

Colonists stand the test

The British commanders were impressed by the Americans' valor. Often they would advance to within ten yards of a British officer in order to get a better shot. They also stood their ground when caught from behind by British flankers. Often though, those same flankers were able to force the rebels out of effective firing range. The events of the day can be considered an American success. The invaders seized no rebel leaders, few stores, and had learned how costly it would be if they continued to venture out of Boston against the Citizen-soldiers who would not give up the fight. After all, the two wagon supply train of the British reinforcements had been captured while still on the road to the combat area by a dozen "old men of Menotomy," a near-by town. Led by an Indian, they ambushed the guard and carried off both the wagons and their supplies. Just think what those brave angry men could have done with better weapons and marksmanship practice.

—Martin K. Gordon
NGB-ICCI-79-4

MARKSMANSHIP: AN EARLY REPORT

BIBLIOGRAPHY

Boatner, Mark M. Encyclopedia of the American Revolution. New York: David McKay Co., Inc., 1966.

Matloff, Maurice, ed. American Military History. Office of the Chief of Military History. Army Historical Series. Washington: Government Printing Office, 1969.

Peckham, Howard. H., ed. The Toll of Independence: Engagements & Battle Casualties of the American Revolution. Chicago: Univ. of Chicago Press, 1974.

Ward, Christopher. The War of the Revolution. 2 vols. New York: The Macmillan Co., 1952.

This essay originally appeared in the January 1979 Push Pin Post

Militiamen Save West Point

Major John Andre was a British officer, who as aide-de-camp to Sir Henry Clinton in New York, was entrusted with handling the secret correspondence between General Clinton and the traitorous American General, Benedict Arnold, at West Point. Captured by accident near Tarrytown, New York in September, 1780, and hung as a spy one month later, Major Andre became the British counterpart to Nathan Hale, the American Revolutionary War patriot.

His captors, volunteer militiamen John Paulding, Isaac Van Wart, and David Williams, were patrolling Pine's Bridge near Tarrytown. Acting under a new state law authorizing temporary patrols of local militia to stop pro-British activities, they were looking for Tories driving cattle to the British lines around New York City, as well as suspected British sympathizers.

Paulding, the group's leader, was still wearing the German coat he had used as a diguise three days earlier while escaping from a British jail. Andre recognized the coat as a German uniform and greeted the Americans as friends. By the time he realized his mistake and displayed his safe-conduct pass from General Arnold, it was too late. He was searched and incriminating documents were discovered. The Americans ignored Andre's bribe offers and escorted him to the post at North Castle.

The rest of the story is well-known. Arnold escaped to the British, but Andre was hanged. The three militiamen who made the arrest and their four companions, who guarded the road, were given a reward of Andre's watch, horse, and bridle. Most importantly, the British were unable to take West Point and split the colonies in half.

This is a reproduction of the Asher Brown Durand oil painting depicting the "Capture of Major Andre" by New York Militiamen. Photo courtesy the Worcester Art Museum, Worcester, Massachusetts, where the original is on display.

Texas Guard Museum On the Move

The National Guard traces its history back to colonial militia units that served in the colonies prior to the American revolution. But, in Texas Guard history recalls the days when the militia was the backbone of the army of a different nation; the Republic of Texas.

Texas militiamen dying at the Alamo and winning their independence at San Jacinto are just two of the displays featured in an exhibit of Texas military history assembled by the Texas Guard. The display is on the road for the entire bicentennial year, throughout Texas.

A feature of the exhibit is a three-screen, multi-media presentation that describes the history of the Guard in Texas. It includes a film clip from the United Artists film, "The Alamo", and a local television production about the battle at San Jacinto.

The exhibit requires 3500 square feet of floor space and is being trucked around the state in two National Guard trucks. It includes paintings, photographs, uniforms, battle flags and other historical items.

The show was officially opened last November, but opened the first of seven road shows in the National Guard Armory in New Braunfels in late January.

Texas School children were among the visitors to the Guard's display of Texas Military History.

MILITIAMEN SAVE WEST POINT
BIBLIOGRAPHY

Bakeless, John E. *Turncoats, Traitors, and Heroes*. Philadelphia: Lippincott, 1960.

Coakley, Robert W., and Conn, Stetson. *The War of the American Revolution: Narrative, Chronology, and Bibliography*. A Bicentennial Publication of the United States Army Center of Military History. Washington: Government Printing Office, 1975.

Lossing, Benson J. *The Pictorial Field Book of the Revolution, or Illustrations by Pen and Pencil, of the History, Biography, Scenery, Relics, and Traditions of the War for Independence*. 2 vols. New York: Harper & Brothers, Publishers, 1851, 1852.

Reprinted several times, this history was especially useful.

Van Doren, Carl C. *Secret History of the American Revolution*. New York: Viking Press, 1941.

Wallace, Willard M. *Traitorous Hero: The Life and Fortunes of Benedict Arnold,* New York: Harper, 1954.

Another useful account.

Winsor, Justin. *Narrative and Critical History of America*. 8 vols. Boston and New York: Houghton, Mifflin, and Company, 1884-1889.

This essay originally appeared in the March 1976 *Push Pin Post*.

Citizen Soldier to Continental Regular: Glover's Marblehead Mariners

Story by Martin K. Gordon

"Washington Crossing the Delaware" if historically inaccurate, still calls to mind one of the more daring military exploits of Major General George Washington. It is usually assumed, correctly by the way, that the black and the white soldiers who manned the oars on the river craft which carried Washington and his army across the Delaware to attack Trenton, New Jersey, on Christmas Day, 1776 were part of his Continental (or regular) Army. What is usually forgotten, however, is that those men were not arbitrarily selected for that duty. Washington knew what he was doing when he selected a regiment which had trained together as militia and worked in their civilian occupations as fishermen on the high seas, sailing from the town of Marblehead, Massachusetts.

The regiment's commanding officer, John Glover, who achieved the rank of Brigadier General shortly after that famous operation, had served in his militia several times before the outbreak of the Revolution. Marblehead was near Essex, the home of the oldest militia establishment in the colonies. Glover's service began in 1759 when he was commissioned as ensign in the Third Foot company in the Fifth County Regiment. Likewise, many of his men had served in the peacetime militia in addition to their civilian work for "Captain" Glover, one of the leading merchants, shipowners, and importers of Marblehead.

In January 1775 the Marblehead militia underwent a political upheaval and emerged thoroughly under the control of the patriotic or revolutionary party. Glover was then elected the regiment's second ranking lieutenant colonel. The new officers accelerated the regimental training to four two-hour drill sessions per week. Most of the able-bodied men in the town turned out for the musters. The British reacted shortly thereafter by attempting to seize the town's military supplies, as they later attempted at Lexington and Concord. They were repulsed by these citizen soldiers. Yet, the militia did not muster that fateful April upon news of the battles around Lexington and Concord. Most of the members of the regiment were out at sea pursuing their livelihoods when that clash took place.

Emanuel Leutze's well-known "Washington Crossing the Delaware" hangs in the Metropolitan Museum of Art in New York City.

Well-disciplined, for the men were used to taking orders from their ship's officers, the regiment was called up for active duty by the colony of Massachusetts May 14, 1775 as the 23d Massachusetts, also known as the Marblehead (Mariner) Regiment, Massachusetts Provincial Army. Lieutenant Colonel Glover, by then the regiment's commanding officer, had ten companies consisting of 505 officers and men under his command at the time. As usually happens in war time the central government, then the Continental Congress, took the regiment into Continental service shortly thereafter, giving Glover a colonel's commission dated July 1, 1775.

With many of the men still wearing their colorful sailor's garb, the regiment soon developed a speciality in what would today be called riverine and amphibious warfare. In August 1776, after service in familiar ships as marines, the Marblehead Mariners participated in the rescue of 9000 American soldiers by ferrying them across New York's East River under cover of darkness after the Americans lost the battle of Long Island. Four months later, those same officers and men, experienced in the ways of rivers and oceans, again ferried Washington's army across a river under cover of darkness, this time to victory.

CITIZEN SOLDIER TO CONTINENTAL REGULAR: GLOVER'S MARBLEHEAD MARINERS

BIBLIOGRAPHY

Billias, George A. *General John Glover and His Marblehead Mariners*. New York: Holt, Rinehart and Winston, 1960.

Elting, John R., Col., ed., *Military Uniforms in America: The Era of the American Revolution, 1755-1795*. From the Series Produced by the Company of Military Historians. San Rafael, CA: Presidio Press, 1974.

See: "14th Continental Regiment (Glover's Marblehead Regiment), 1775-1776."

Higginbotham, Don. *The War of American Independence: Military Attitudes, Policies, and Practice, 1763-1789*. The Macmillan Wars of the United States Series. New York: The Macmillan Company, 1971.

Kaplan, Sidney. *The Black Presence in the Era of the American Revolution*. New York: New York Graphic Society, Ltd., in Association with the Smithsonian Institution Press, 1973.

Quarles, Benjamin. *The Negro in the American Revolution*. New York: W. W. Norton & Company, Inc., 1973.

ERRATA

In paragraph two, Marblehead is in Essex County. Also, John Glover's service should read Third Company, 5th Essex Regiment.

In paragraph four, the 1775 designation should be Glover's Regiment. It was redesignated 1 January 1776 as the 14th Continental Regiment.

This essay originally appeared in the June 1976 *Push Pin Post*.

Those Devils in Baggy Pants

The American militia units who adopted the Zouave drill are mainly remembered today for their funny-looking uniforms. Those uniforms, however, formed a key part of the unusual and interesting drill of some of the most famous militia units of the pre- and post-Civil War years. The Zouaves caught the eye of the American public during the Crimean War years of 1854–1856. The name came from a mountain tribe in Algeria, the Zouaves, whose soldiers had a special method of fighting which made them remarkably effective. They were so successful against the French, that the French Army adapted their system of fighting to entire regiments that were also called Zouaves. The key features of the drill were the bright uniforms and the special tactics they used on the drill and battle fields.

To be understood, the uniforms must be contrasted against the tight-fitting clothes of the times. The scarlet trousers were loose and baggy, and the dark blue, gold-trimmed jacket and blue shirt had no collars in order that the Zouaves could do their exacting maneuvers with the necessary freedom of motion. The distinctive and demanding Zouave drill previewed and perhaps influenced the later regular army development of the fire team. At a time when most standard drill manuals did not even provide for squad-level tactics, the basic Zouave maneuver unit was a four-man squad. Those men drilled until they became one individual with eyes and arms on all four sides. Their drills taught them to load and fire on the run, while lying down, or kneeling. They were perfected in the art of the bayonet and executed their steps at an incredible rate of action.

One eager young militiaman was responsible for the spread of interest in that romantic Algerian-French system which helped to revitalize the American militia on the eve of the Civil War. Elmer Ephraim Ellsworth was born 11 April 1837 at Malta, New York and attended school at nearby Mechanicsville. He moved around and, after settling in Chicago, began taking fencing lessons from a former surgeon of a French Zouave regiment. Under his fencing master's tutelage, Ellsworth translated and mastered the Zouave drill manuals. He tried out those new drill systems on the students in the gymnasium classes he was conducting. Word of his new and different drills spread in militia circles. His reputation grew and soon he became commanding officer of the National Guard Cadets of Chicago, later changed to the U.S. Zouave Cadets. He was concerned that war was approaching, and worked both to increase his unit's efficiency and to make the general public more aware of the need for an improved militia.

In the spring and early summer of 1860, Ellsworth and his company made a tour of the major eastern cities presenting their drills. The complete Zouave drill of over 500 movements took about four and a half hours to complete. The Zouaves either drilled alone, sometimes on stage, or against local militia units. The tour was a fantastic success and Zouave units sprang up all over the country. Other units took a new interest in their drill and uniforms.

Ellsworth returned from his tour to work in the law office of Abraham Lincoln. Becoming a close personal friend of the future President, Ellsworth campaigned for him during the 1860 elections. He accompanied Lincoln to Washington after the election as his personal bodyguard. Ellsworth's goal was to have Lincoln establish a militia bureau in the War Department with himself as head of it. There, he could work to prepare the militia for the approaching conflict. While he was working on those proposals, the Civil War came. Ellsworth, eager for action, accepted a commission as colonel in the New York State Militia. He organized a regiment from among the volunteer firemen of New York City, the Eleventh New York, known as the Fire Zouaves. The regiment rushed to Washington to help defend the capital. They were a rambunctious group, loyal to their colonel but not interested in obeying orders from anyone else.

While in Washington, they helped put out a fire in the downtown district when the local fire companies were slow to respond. The Fire Zouaves were chosen to participate in the first Union offensive of the war: the capture of Alexandria and the land on the Virginia side of the Potomac River opposite Washington. The Confederates retreated in the face of the superior Union forces. Ellsworth's regiment began the occupation of Alexandria. Ellsworth was leading a small party through the city when he saw a Confederate flag flying from the Marshall House, a local hotel. He led his party to the roof to cut it down. Returning down the stairs with the flag, the men were surprised by the proprietor, James W. Jackson, who killed Ellsworth before anyone could react.

E. E. Ellsworth, the first Union officer to die in action in the Civil War, was mourned throughout the Union. The cry "Remember Ellsworth" became the battle cry of the Eleventh New York, and Ellsworth Zouaves sprang up throughout the remaining states. In death as in life, Ellsworth, with his unusual uniform, proved to be an inspiration to the American militia.

—Martin K. Gordon

Library of Congress

A contemporary lithograph showing the slaying of Ellsworth, 24 May 1861

THOSE DEVILS IN BAGGY PANTS

BIBLIOGRAPHY

Brown, Anne S. K. "Some San Francisco Uniforms of 1870." *Military Collector & Historian* 4 (March 1952): 1-7.

   Discusses Zouave units after the Civil War.

Cooling, B. Franklin. *Symbol, Sword, and Shield: Defending Washington During the Civil War.* Hamden, CT: Archon Books, 1975.

Hill, Jim Dan. *The Minute Man in Peace and War: A History of the National Guard.* Harrisburg, PA: Stackpole Co., 1964.

Leech, Margaret. *Reville in Washington, 1860-1865.* New York: Time, Inc., 1962 Reprint of 1941 ed.

McAfee, Michael J. *Zouaves...The First and the Bravest: European and American Zouave Uniforms, Accoutrements, and Works of Art from the Collections of the West Point Museum.* West Point Museum Bulletin No. 4. West Point: United States Military Academy, 1979.

   An important contribution to Zouave studies published after "Those Devils in Baggy Pants."

McBarron, H. Charles, and Todd, Frederick. "United States Zouave Cadets, 1859-1860." *Military Collector & Historian* 3 (September 1951): 71-72.

   Discusses the Ellsworth Zouaves.

Ney, Virgil. *Organization and Equipment of the Infantry Rifle Squad: From Valley Forge to ROAD.* Combat Operations Research Group Memorandum CORG-M-194, January 1965. Available under Defense Technical Information Center Order No. 461439.

   Pages six through thirteen discuss Civil War era infantry drill tactics.

Randall, Ruth P. *Colonel Elmer Ellsworth: A Biography of Lincoln's Friend and First Hero of the Civil War.* Boston: Little, Brown and Co., 1960.

Todd, Frederick P. "Ellsworth's Campaign Uniform." *Military Collector & Historian* 5 (March 1953): 19-22.

This essay originally appeared in the March 1977 *Push Pin Post*.

"I bowed briefly on the grim corregidor"

As Japan was mobilizing in 1940 to attack the United States, the National Guard was mobilizing to defend it. In August 1940, President Franklin D. Roosevelt ordered the Guard into active federal service. Between September 16, 1940 and October 6, 1941, the National Guard brought into federal service more than 300,000 men. Among those men in their organized units were three that were destined to create a unique place in Guard history, a place that is immortalized in the Creed of the Guard: "I bowed briefly on the grim Corregidor."

In one of the last photographs out of Bataan, this soldier is preparing a Molotov Cocktail for an approaching Japanese tank.

Typically, the Guardsmen came from different parts of the country to perform their common defensive mission. One of the units, still in existence as the 200th Air Defense Artillery, NM, was originally organized in April 1883 as the Second Cavalry Battalion, New Mexico Volunteer Militia. When it was inducted into federal service January 6, 1941, though, it was under its six-months' old designation as the 200th Coast Artillery (Anti-aircraft). That regiment arrived in the Philippine Islands in September 1941 at Fort Stotsenburg, about 50 miles north of Manila, to protect the key air base at Clark Field. The morning of December 8, about 30 officers, 500 enlisted men and 40 vehicles were detached to put into operation anti-aircraft artillery around Manila. That unit later became the 515th Coast Artillery. These units were equipped with 3-inch and 37mm guns, .50-caliber machine guns, and searchlights. The vertical range of the 3-inchers was 27,000 feet. The 200th was in action against Japanese aviation almost daily from the start of the war to the regiment's surrender on April 9, 1942. By that date, it had been credited with 51 enemy kills. On December 8, Japanese bombers flying in formation at 22,000 to 25,000 feet bombed Clark Field. Firing ammunition made in 1932 and earlier years, the frustrated artillerymen fired a lot of duds that day, perhaps only one out of every six shells exploded.

Also in the action that day were two National Guard tank battalions. The 192d had been constituted as a battalion only a year earlier, with companies from Wisconsin, Illinois, Ohio and Kentucky. The 194th, still in existence as Minnesota's 194th Cavalry, was formed from Minnesota, Missouri, and California tank companies. Just as the 200th was defending Clark Field, the 194th (minus Company B which had been sent to Alaska), was on the alert at the field in case of Japanese airborne infantry landings. The 192d was in reserve at Fort Stotsenburg. Both battalions had arrived in the Philippines that fall. All three units, artillerymen and tankers, were to fight together that fall.

The 200th fought in defense of Clark Field until the withdrawal of the ground forces towards Bataan and Corregidor forced it also to displace to the rear. It provided anti-aircraft defenses for a number of key river crossings and bridges. Ammunition restrictions caused a limit of three rounds per target to be placed on both the 200th and 515th. The 200th later assumed responsibility for defending Bataan airfield.

The tank battalions conducted fighting withdrawals to Bataan. Prewar United States planning had called for American and Filipino forces to withdraw to Bataan and Corregidor early in the conflict to deny the use of the great Manila harbor to the enemy. Implementation of these plans fell short in the critical area of supply, however. These withdrawals were accomplished by men on half-rations, short of necessary medicines such as quinine, and operating without adequate relief or replacements. The tanks regularly had to operate without infantry support. There were incidents such as the platoon from the 192nd that was sent that December to attack and ran into a perfect tank trap. The Guardsmen in column on a narrow road could neither fight nor turn around once the lead tank was knocked out by the 47mm guns that could cut through the tanks of the day.

Inevitably, the combat efficiency of the men wore down. The end came on April 8-9 for the Luzon Force, the 78,000 American and Filipino soldiers, sailors, and airmen on Bataan that included the Guard units. By then the 200th had been bombed out of its positions, and after destroying its specialized equipment, was functioning as the only organized infantry unit available to form a defensive line against the Japanese assault in the II Corps sector of Bataan peninsula. Malnutrition and disease had been major problems for the overworked men and now most of them could no longer fight. Meanwhile on April 7 and 8, the two Companies A of the 192nd and 194th, functioning as beach defense units, stopped a Japanese landing behind the American lines.

There are no careful records written in the last days of a major defeat, but it might be assumed that the 200th Coast Artillery fighting as infantry and the two tank battalions of the National Guard fired what must be among the last shots of the army of Bataan, the Luzon Force, before its surrender of April 9. Estimates of the number of military survivors to reach Corregidor island range between 2,000 and 2,800. Their efforts were in vain. Largely too exhausted to contribute to the defense of the fortress, they could only join in its surrender less than a month later.

March 3, 1945, the National Guard's 37th Division, working with regular Army units, overcame the last Japanese resistance in Manila. One month short of three years, the National Guard returned victorious to the island of Luzon.

—Martin K. Gordon

"I BOWED BRIEFLY ON THE GRIM CORREGIDOR"
BIBLIOGRAPHY

Baldwin, Hanson W. <u>Battles Lost and Won: Great Campaigns of World War II</u>. New York: Harper & Row, Pubs., 1966.

    See Chapter IV, "'The Rock'--The Fall of Corregidor."

Belote, James H. and Belote, William H. <u>Corregidor: The Saga of a Fortress</u>. New York: Harper & Row, Pubs., 1967.

Gordon, Sol, Lt. Col., and Tenneill, Clint, Jr., Capt. <u>National Guard Almanac</u>. Washington, DC: Uniformed Services Almanac, Inc., 1977.

Miller, Ernest B. <u>Bataan Uncensored</u>. Long Prairie, MN: The Hart Publications, Inc., 1949.

    A history of the 194th Tank Battalion critical of General MacArthur and the Regular Army staffs in the Philippines.

Morton, Louis. <u>The Fall of the Philippines</u>. United States Army in World War II: The War in the Pacific Series. Washington: Government Printing Office, 1953.

"Report of Operations of USAFFE and USFIP in the Philippine Islands, 1941-1942 (J. M. Wainwright, General, USA, Former Commanding General USFIP: May 1946), Annex X, Philippine Provisional Coast Artillery Brigade: Groupment "A."

    A copy of this history of the National Guard Coast Artillery in the Philippines is on file in the U. S. Army Center of Military History.

U. S. Army. Center of Military History. Organizational History Branch. "Unit Files: 192d Tank Battalion, 194th Cavalry, 200th Air Defense Artillery."

This essay originally appeared in the November 1978 <u>Push Pin Post</u>.

Operation BOB CAT: The National Guard on Bora Bora

BACKGROUND

The BOB CAT Task Force, originally code named Advance Base Blueberry, was born shortly after the attack on Pearl Harbor, on Christmas Day, 1941. On that day Admiral Ernest J. King asked his planners to study possible fueling bases in the central South Pacific area for supply ships. This southern route to Australia and New Zealand was needed as a line of supply that could go around the fast advancing Japanese Navy.

Five days later the decision was made to establish the base at Bora Bora in the Society Islands, then under control of the Free French government. A seaplane base, a fuel depot for both fuel oil and gasoline, and an Army garrison of 3,500 men were planned for that attractive south seas backwater island which had a permanent population of under 1400 Polynesian and French settlers. Pre-war contingency planning had called for the Marines to defend these island supply depots. But the Marines were already stretched thin and so the National Guard was called upon to furnish the infantry and artillerymen necessary for a defense against expected Japanese raiders. The 102d Infantry (Second Connecticut), constituted June 26, 1672, and minus two battalions, supplied the infantry. The 198th Coast Artillery (now the 198th Signal Battalion, the First Delaware), constituted December 9, 1775, supplied part of the artillery. One of the Regular Army artillerymen on the island, Captain Phillip Wehle, came from the same Norwalk, Connecticut area as did the Connecticut Guardsmen, a factor which might have helped the various military and naval forces achieve their high level of harmony.

THE OCCUPATION

One of the principal values of the BOB CAT operation was that both the Army and the Navy learned how to plan and carry out island operations better in the future. The ships were not loaded properly so some of the equipment needed to help the unloading was under the gear it was supposed to help move. There were too many combat troops for the number of supporting personnel so that the infantry and artillerymen had to work at unloading the ships as well as at their own tasks. Important construction equipment had been left in the states while, as it developed, the light roads on the island could not bear the weight of the heavy American construction and towing vehicles. The anticipated water supply, based on a 90 year-old French map, proved to be non-existent, so that had to be built. Fortunately, the Japanese did not attack, either while this confusion was being sorted out, or even later in the war when the island defenses were finally organized.

LIFE ON THE ISLAND

Retired Marine Corps Brigadier General Joseph Earnshaw, the one Marine in the operation, recently described the relations between the various services: "There may have been some differences of opinion, but as far as relations between the National Guard and regulars, between the Army and the Navy, every one worked in harmony in setting up the island defenses and the fuel oil depots. Every one worked so hard they may have been too tired to fight . . . every one was a 'Bob-Cat.'" General Earnshaw then pointed out that the men had had to haul, slide, and push their 7" naval guns and their mounts up a 42° slope in order to be able to overlook the harbor with their weapons.

The soldiers at first spent sleepless nights waiting for the Japanese landing they kept expecting. The tropical climate of steamy heat, heavy rainfall, and the resultant mud soon gave the soldiers something else to think about. As they recited in the "Bobcat Blues":

Of course there were soggy dripping skies
And also mosquitoes, ants and flies.
We did not disturb them as gaily they played
'Cause believe it or not they had us outweighed.

The island forces had a library of 900 volumes. They could only, in the first years, see movies when they borrowed them from passing ships, and mail took six weeks to reach the states via cargo vessels. As the construction was completed, the combat forces fell into a routine of firing all weapons regularly as two per-cent of the ammunition on hand was allowed for target practice each month.

THE WAR CONTINUES

As the fuel depot's resupply mission became routine, the soldiers became increasingly bored. American naval victories had reduced the Japanese threat to supply lines. The Delaware 198th moved on in February 1943, six months after it had been alerted to leave, for action in the New Hebrides, Solomons, and

A gun of the 198th Coast Artillery (First Delaware) being hauled to the top of a ridge on Bora Bora. (NAVY Dept. Photo (National Archives))

Philippine Islands. While the other battalions of the Connecticut 102d fought in Europe, this part of the regiment performed both combat and garrison duty in the Pacific for the remainder of the war. Bora Bora had served as a training ground for later operations as well as a practical laboratory where the problems of island operations and construction were met and solved, often by the backbreaking labor of the rank and file soldier.

—Martin K. Gordon

OPERATION BOB CAT:

THE NATIONAL GUARD ON BORA BORA

BIBLIOGRAPHY

PUBLISHED SOURCES

Ballantine, Duncan S. U. S. Naval Logistics in the Second World War. Princeton: Princeton Univ. Press, 1949.

Leighton, Richard M. and Coakley, Robert W. Global Logistics and Strategy, 1940-1943. The United States Army in World War II: The War Department Series. Washington: Government Printing Office, 1955.

U. S. Navy. Bureau of Yards and Docks. Building the Navy's Bases in World War II: History of the Bureau of Yards and Docks and the Civil Engineer Corps, 1940-1946. vol. 2. Washington: Government Printing Office, 1947.

UNPUBLISHED SOURCES

Earnshaw, Joseph W., Brig. Gen., USMC, Ret. "Correspondence with the author and personal papers relating to OPERATION BOB CAT."

Copies of General Earnshaw's letters and papers, including the full text of the "Bobcat Blues," have been deposited in the Marine Corps Historical Center, Washington, DC 20374.

The author acknowledges with gratitude the assistance of General Earnshaw in the preparation of this essay. He is quoted therein with his permission.

Marolda, Edward J. "Manning the South Pacific Rear Base: Military Life on Bora Bora in Early World War II."

The author acknowledges with gratitude the assistance of Mr. Edward Marolda in the preparation of this essay. A copy of his paper is on file in the Naval Historical Center, Washington, DC 20374.

U. S. Army. Organizational History Branch. "Unit Files: 198th Signal Bn (1st Delaware); 102d Infantry (2d Connecticut); Co. "A," 2d Bn, 102d Infantry."

_____. Archives Branch. "Biographical Files: Wehle, Phillip."

_____. Archives Branch. "Geographic File: P. Bora Bora. 370.2, BOBCAT Task Force."

U. S. Navy. Naval Operational Archives. "Folder: Bora Bora, Society Islands."

This essay originally appeared in the May 1979 Push Pin Post.

NEBRASKA TAKES TO THE SKIES

The development of the modern Air National Guard can be divided into three historical phases. The first marks the pioneering years before the First World War; the second the inter-war years of the observation squadrons, and the third the post-World War II recognition and growth of the Air National Guard of today.

Nebraska's Air Guardsmen have participated in this process from the beginning. Several state guard forces had small air branches by 1916, but with the exception of New York, none of them were adequately supported. The pioneering airmen of the Nebraska NG are typical of this period. Their work came close to being a one-man, one-plane operation.

It all began in 1913 when the officers and men of Nebraska's Signal Corps assembled a biplane at Fremont. It was a purchased Curtiss Aeroplane Model D. It had no fuselage, had an engine mounted between the wings driving a pusher propeller, and was fitted with three wheels. The pilot sat on an exposed seat ahead of the wings. This plane participated in the Guard's annual encampment.

The first formal acknowledgement of this budding aviation section came in 1915 when Captain Castle W. Schaffer was made chief of aviation. Shortly after, Ralph E. McMillen, a qualified pilot, enlisted and was commissioned a captain in this small group. Both men furnished their own airplanes. This was fairly typical of the pioneering period. Pilots trained as best they could and equipment came from a variety of sources.

In 1915 the question of funds for a new flying branch was raised with the governor. He advised the aviators to give exhibitions at county fairs and other public gatherings to raise money to supplement their small state appropriations. The two pilots attempted to do this during that summer and fall. Captain Schaffer encountered difficulties because of the poor condition of his airplane. At the county fair at Julesburg, Colo., he made one successful flight and then took off on a second one. As he attempted to come down, the eager crowd filled his landing place, and he had to land in an adjacent field where rough ground flipped over the airplane and heavily damaged the wing sections. Schaffer may have given up flying following this accident, for all official flights during that summer were done by Captain McMillen, and Schaffer's name does not appear in the October list of officers successfully passing the Guard course of instruction and examination for 1915. McMillen also had a few accidents that summer but none of them were major.

On July 15, 1915, the Nebraska NG officially organized an Aviation Corps

The Curtiss Model D was built by members of the Signal Corps Aviation Section of the Nebraska National Guard in Fremont in 1913. (Photo by Nebraska National Guard)

with headquarters at the state fairgrounds in Lincoln. Its insignia was the same "as that for the Signal Corps, with the exception that attached to the crossed flags and torch there shall be silver wings for both dress and service uniforms for the collar devices," the activating order read. On Sunday August 15, 1915, McMillen, while on active duty at summer camp with the 4th Infantry, experimented with bombs dropped from the air, certainly a forward-looking concept.

The day before, the flying strength of the section had been doubled when Edgar W. "Happy" Bagnell was commissioned a first lieutenant in the Nebraska NG Aviation Corps. Bagnell was to become the first Nebraska aviator to receive an Army pilot certificate in 1916. McMillen had been declared medically ineligible because he had broken both legs in a 1912 accident. Bagnell accepted a commission in the Army's Signal Officers Reserve Corps and participated in the First World War in that capacity. Meanwhile, McMillen had died in a crash while flying in a display at St. Francis, Kan., on September 2, 1916. With Schaffer gone, McMillen dead, and Bagnell in the reserves, the Nebraska Aero Company, as it had been renamed, faded out of existence by the start of World War I. It had never owned an airplane in its own name.

In the between-the-wars years all Guard aviation units, with but one exception before 1939, were assigned as divisional observation squadrons. That exception was the 154th Observation Squadron, Little Rock, Ark. which was designated non-divisional and assigned to the VII Corps Headquarters. The 109th Observation Squadron, St. Paul, Minn., the first squadron to be federally recognized after the war, met the aviation needs of the 34th Division. That was the division to which Nebraska's Guardsmen had been attached during World War I.

The Cornhusker State resumed its active role in the development in the Air Guard in the third current phase of ANG history. The nation's first ANG unit, the 120th Fighter Squadron of Colorado, was granted federal recognition on June 30, 1946. Nebraska barely missed that distinction, because its 173rd Fighter Squadron was federally recognized in Lincoln, Neb., July 26 of the same year. The assigned aircraft included 22 F-51 "Mustangs." The squadron was one of the first three ANG units to be converted to jet aircraft (the F-80 "Shooting Star") and was officially reorganized as a Fighter Squadron Jet Propelled Aug. 1, 1948. The ANG has since undergone several reorganizations in equipment, designation, and mission. Service has included active duty during the Korean War, the Berlin Crisis, Vietnam, as well as continual training exercises.

Today, the men and women of Nebraska's 155th Tactical Reconnaissance Group with their RF-4 Phantoms continue the more than 60-year old participation of Cornhuskers in the Air National Guard.

—Martin K. Gordon

NEBRASKA TAKES TO THE SKIES

BIBLIOGRAPHY

Casari, Robert B. "The Aviation Corps of the Nebraska National Guard, 1915-1917." Nebraska History 56 (Spring 1975): 1-19.

    The general background parts of this article must be used with caution.

Colby, Elbridge. The National Guard of the United States: A Half Century of Progress. Manhattan, KS: Military Affairs/ Aerospace Historian Publishing Series, 1977.

    See Chapter IX, "Building the Modern National Guard."

Hill, Jim Dan. The Minute Man in Peace and War: A History of the National Guard. Harrisburg, PA: Stackpole Co., 1964.

Larkins, William T. "Aircraft History of the National Guard: Part 1 - Pre-War." American Aviation Historical Society Journal. 1 (April-June 1956): 27-32, 40.

National Guard Alamanac. Ed. by Capt. Clint Tennill, Jr., ARNG, and Lt. Col. Sol Gordon, USAF (Ret.). Washington: Uniformed Services Almanac, Inc., 1977.

Nebraska. National Guard. Nebraska Army & Air National Guard History, 1854-1957. Lincoln: Adjutant General's Dept., 1957.

This essay originally appeared in the July 1978 Push Pin Post.

MUCH BETTER LATE THAN NEVER
ANGR 210-3

Your history is a fairly complex subject. The long history behind the National Guard of today is, like love, a many splendored thing. For example, the Air National Guard can be examined from at least three different levels. At the federal level, 1916 is a good year to study. As the Mexican Border crisis was building, the War Department asked Congress for more money than it had originally intended to request. It asked for $9,640,800 to organize twelve National Guard aviation squadrons and $3,440,866 for regular Army squadrons. The final bill, however, only approved the $76,000 for the future ANG that had been in the pre-crisis budget. That year the federal government supported the Guard's aviation program only to the extent that it could purchase four airplanes and train fifty officers throughout the entire country.

At the state level, the 1915 case of Nebraska, shows the early problems of aviation in the Guard. That was the year that the state's governor advised the new flying branch of the Nebraska National Guard that the aviators should give exhibitions at county fairs and other public gatherings to raise money to supplement their small state appropriation.

The historical situation at the local level is glimpsed in the April 1925 accomplishments of the Washington, National Guard's 116th Observation Squadron. That month the squadron's three JN "Jennies" arrived in a box car completely disassembled and without any instructions on how to put them together. Some long days followed as the Spokane Guardsmen experimented with various ways of fitting the parts together. Finally, they completed the work and the airplanes actually flew. Then the orders came grounding the "Jennies" unless the flight personnel wore parachutes. Some time after the order, the necessary design instructions arrived explaining how to rebuild the upper wings so that the pilot could use his parachute. Last of all came the parachutes.

Members of New York's First Aero Company complete a trail-blazing cross country flight from Mineola, N.Y., to Princeton, N.J. in 1916.—*(National Guard Heritage Series)*

One can only wonder about how many similar insights into the years of work that brought about today's Air Guard were lost for lack of an ANG Regulation 210-3, "Air National Guard Historical Program." But the development of the Air Guard continues. Although the Regulation would have been useful years ago, at least it is here for the future. The story of the men and women will now be better written and better preserved than it has been.

This author left one important part of Guard history out of his 1977 column, "Its Your History Too," which was about the important role you can play in preserving the heritage of the minuteman. What was left out of that column is this month's subject: the role of official historical reports. The official unit historical report (NGB Form 114 for the ANG) is not just another burden placed on field units. It is the basis of how you and your work will be remembered in future years. You are not writing it just to keep the new ANG Office of History (ANG/HO) happy. The Attachment to ANGR 210-3 states that the authors of the new reports should keep in mind the reader 10 years from now. The above examples from 1915, 1916, and 1925, should indicate that the new reports will be useful for many years to come if those who write the reports do a good job. And that is the key to the success of the program. If you now take the use of the form its possible appendices as your method of properly recording both the routines and changes in your unit that are the heart of its activities, you will have helped both yourself and those to come.

It is an obvious fact of history that historians can only study that which is available for them to study. In other words, if you do not properly record and preserve your history, the civilian and military writers who study the ANG will simply have to omit your activities from their work. They cannot work without sources. We do not know, of course, which of today's or tomorrow's events will be as important as the November 1916 flight illustrated on this page. But we do know that with the new Office of History, when events happen, their record will be preserved—if you cooperate.

—Martin K. Gordon

MUCH BETTER LATE THAN NEVER: ANGR 210-3

BIBLIOGRAPHY

Casari, Robert B. "The Aviation Corps of the Nebraska National Guard, 1915-1917." Nebraska History 56 (Spring 1975): 1-19.

The general background parts of this article must be used with caution.

Larkins, William T. "Aircraft History of the National Guard: Part 1 - Pre-War." American Aviation Historical Society Journal. 1 (April-June 1956): 27-32, 40.

ERRATUM

A word was omitted from the printed title of this essay. It should read "Much Better Late Than Never: ANGR 210-3."

This essay originally appeared in the March 1978 Push Pin Post.

1736: The Guard's One Hundredth Year

Although the American colonies were at war for one-third of the first 156 years of the colonial period, the decade of the one hundredth anniversary of the National Guard was a relatively calm one. However, although calm in terms of combat, it was still an active period in the history of the Guard.

In the South, in particular, several different activities with long-reaching consequences began in the decade of 1736. Georgia was founded in 1733 and three years later began developing Guard-related activities that have endured. Fort Frederica, the remains of which are now a national park, was built in 1736 as a base against the Spanish to the South. When on the offensive, it served as a jumping off point for the English militia, regulars, and their Indian allies. In 1742, the fort and its defenders blocked the last significant Spanish attempt to dislodge the Georgia settlers. Also in Georgia, the ninth oldest unit in today's National Guard, Service Battery, 2nd Battalion, 214th Field Artillery, Georgia ARNG was activated February 13, 1736 as the English Troop of Rangers, also known as the Georgia Rangers and Horsemen.

South Carolina's militia was in ferment and change throughout the decade. As a result of changes in the population, colonists arrived in the colony to settle Indian and Spanish war scares, and fear of slave uprisings. The white population declined in the early 1730s to the extent that the militia might have dropped as low as 1,500 potential militiamen. But that trend was soon reversed. In November 1732, the first group of Swiss colonists arrived in the colony to settle along the Savannah River about 30 miles from its mouth. More Swiss followed and ultimately a Swiss regiment of militia was formed. By the end of 1733, with the activation of regiments of foot in Craven and Granville Counties, the colony had five organized regiments. In February 1737, upon receipt of reports of an impending Spanish attack, one hundred militiamen were called up and sent to Port Royal. The force reached 270 by March 19 and was demobilized during May when no unusual Spanish activity was reported in either Cuba or Florida.

During the Yamassee Indian War of 1717, several hundred black citizen soldiers were called up to help the white militiamen defeat the Indians. But conditions changed rapidly in the colony. The Militia Act of 1721 merged the slave patrols into the militia system, partially because able-bodied young men were using participation in slave patrols as an excuse to avoid militia duty. After a serious slave insurrection in 1739, the Carolinians were afraid to arm the black inhabitants of the colony. This decade marked changes in the South Carolina militia which were to have an impact up to the Civil War.

Another current militia unit, the 1st Battalion, 201st Field Artillery, West Virginia ARNG, was activated in that decade. The unit began in 1735 as the Militia of Berkeley County, Virginia.

Further to the North, the "border wars" between Maryland and Pennsylvania were fought in 1734. These clashes were fought not only by roaming armed bands, but at least on the Maryland side, the sheriffs, who were leading the actions, organized their posses out of the local militia. Those were the fights that led to the surveying of the Mason-Dixon Line.

In Massachusetts, a leading manual of the decade, based on an English model, was published in 1733. Titled *Militia Discipline: The Words of Command, and Directions....*, the Boston publisher added sections on how to drill a company and a battalion and on the militia laws of Massachusetts. The book was a ready reference for the commander of a unit on Muster Day. It was at least the third militia manual published in Massachusetts. That colony, facing threats from both the Indians and the French, had already organized four units by the 1730s that are still in existence today and was to activate a fifth such unit in 1741. Those units are the 1st Battalion, 182nd Infantry, (activated as the 1st Regiment of Middlesex); the 101st Engineer Battalion, (activated as the Militia Regiment of Essex County); the 772nd Military Police Company, (activated as the 1st Foot Company, 3rd Regiment of Militia, Bristol County); the 1st and 2nd Battalions, 104th Infantry, (activated as the Militia Regiments of Hampshire and Berkshire Counties). The unit, activated in 1741, that just missed this anniversary is the 126th Signal Battalion, then designated as the Independent Company of Cadets.

Thus, it can be seen that even in the relatively peaceful centennial decade of the Guard, it was a needed force in the then colonies.

—Martin K. Gordon

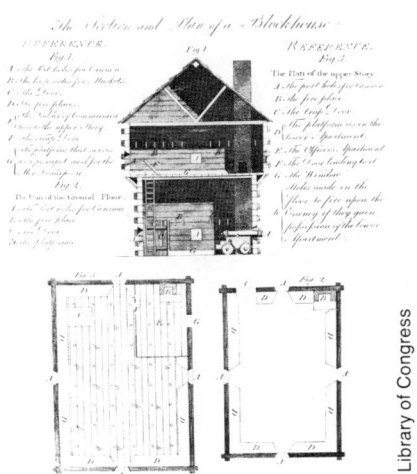

This blockhouse fort plan from the early 1700s is typical of the defensive fortifications standing by for use by the citizen soldier in time of emergency.

1736: THE GUARD'S ONE HUNDREDTH YEAR

BIBLIOGRAPHY

Henry, Howell M. *The Police Control of the Slave in South Carolina*. Published 1914. Reprint ed., New York: Negro Universities Press, 1968.

Leach, Douglas E. *Arms for Empire: A Military History of the British Colonies in North America, 1607-1763*. The Macmillan Wars of the United States Series. New York: The Macmillan Co., 1971.

McMaster, Fitzhugh. *Soldiers and Uniforms: South Carolina Military Affairs, 1670-1775*. Tricentennial Booklet No. 10. Columbia, SC: Published for the South Carolina Tricentennial Commission by the University of South Carolina Press, 1971.

Militia Discipline: The Words of Command and Directions for Exercising the Musket, Bayonet, & Carthridge.... Boston: Printed for D. Henchman, at the corner Shop over against the Brick-Meeting-House in Cornhil, 1733; reprint ed., East Winthrop, Maine: Museum Research Associates, 1975.

Peckham, Howard H. *The Colonial Wars, 1689-1762*. The Chicago History of American Civilization Series. Chicago: Univ. of Chicago Press, 1964.

Sarles, Frank B., Jr. and Shedd, Charles E. *Colonials and Patriots: Historic Places Commemorating our Forebears, 1700-1783*. National Park Service National Survey of Historic Sites and Buildings. Washington: Government Printing Office, 1964.

Scharf, J. Thomas. *History of Maryland from the Earliest Period to the Present Day*. 3 vols. Baltimore: Pub. by John B. Piet, 1879.

Shy, John. *A People Numerous and Armed: Reflections on the Military Struggle for Independence*. New York: Oxford Univ. Press, 1976.

U. S. Army. Center of Military History. "Revolutionary War Unit Ceremony Participants," and "Revolutionary War Unit Ceremony Listing of the 31 Army Units in Continuous Existence."

Lists of National Guard units that participated in the American Revolution which were still in existence in 1976.

This essay originally appeared in the October 1978 *Push Pin Post*

1836: The Guard's Two Hundredth Year

The decade of the two hundredth anniversary of the National Guard was marked by turmoil in which outlines of the twentieth century Guard can be seen emerging from the events of those days.

COMPULSORY DRILL

The continuing decline in the enrolled militia was one problem. There were two types of militia before the Civil War: the enrolled in which every able-bodied white male was liable for call-up for militia duty; and the volunteer units whose members drilled more than the required number of days and who paid for their own sometimes elaborate uniforms and equipment. The enrolled militia became the basis for the pools of draft-eligible manpower while the volunteer units have evolved into today's National Guard. The 1830s saw a decline in general interest in the compulsory militia musters, increasing resistance to paying the fines for non-attendance, and a growing realization that the less than five drill days per year that most states required was leaving those militiamen who attended with little practical training because half of each of those few days was usually taken up with record-keeping chores.

Credit: Library of Congress
Many volunteer units had special marches dedicated to them. The covers of the sheet music depict the colorful uniforms of the citizen-soldier of the 1830s. This 1836 quick step was composed in honor of and dedicated to the New York Light Guards and the Boston Light Infantry.

THE VOLUNTEERS

In spite of that problem, the volunteer militia grew and the cities and states found good uses for their militia forces. As the cities expanded, so did the volunteer companies that were often organized around a neighborhood, a church, a volunteer fire company, or a common ethnic background. The ethnic flavor of the militia can be seen in such unit names as Catalanos, Jaegers, Voltigeurs, Highlanders, and Hibernia Greens. Other volunteers either invoked their earlier arrival in this country or, at the other extreme, identified with their new homeland with such unit names as "American," "Jefferson," or "Washington."

The New Orleans black militia units had disappeared, though, in spite of the general growth in ethnic companies. There were three reasons for this disorganization of old companies: 1) its leaders were preoccupied with business successes and had less time for military activities; 2) they did not want to become involved in the growing controversy over slavery and the use of the militia in controlling the slaves; and 3) the increasingly prejudiced state legislature repealed the authorizing legislation for the Battalion of Chosen Men of Color. No other state had even permitted black participation as much as had Louisiana.

Elaborate uniforms also marked the emerging volunteer militia. Before the British discovery of the value of Khaki in the 1850s, all military forces tended towards bright uniforms that would be impressive on the parade ground and reflect favorably on the cause the force was intended to defend. Some units such as the Trojan Greens of Troy, New York, took their names from their uniforms. That unit was succeeded by 1835 by the Troy Citizens Corps. Although those citizen soldiers abandoned green for red full dress uniforms after the Civil War, their unit has continued in existence and is today Company C, 1st Battalion, 210th Armor. Another example of a current unit dating from that era is the 141st Artillery, organized 7 September 1838 in the Louisiana Militia as the Washington Artillery Company at New Orleans.

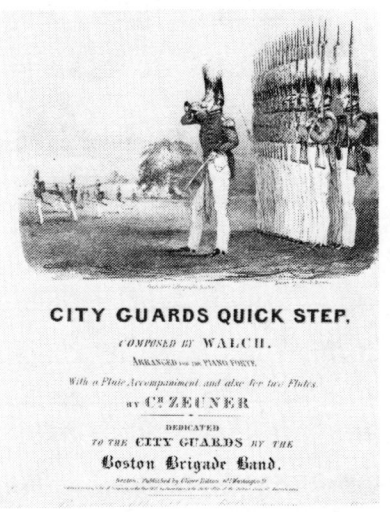

Credit: Library of Congress
This march shows the Boston City Guards drilling on Boston Common, the historic drilling site of the Boston militia. The march was written in 1835.

ACTION

But the volunteers did more than muster and drill. Brevet Major General Edmund P. Gaines, USA, then on the Texas-United States border, asked, April 1836, the governor of Louisiana for a brigade of volunteer militia and the governors of Tennessee, Kentucky, Alabama, and Mississippi for a regiment each of mounted volunteers. He planned to use the 10,000 men to move into Texas territory to protect the United States while the War for Texas Independence, raged. The states acted promptly but President Andrew Jackson, himself a former militiaman, countermanded the orders because he saw no need for the projected maneuver.

Domestically, the militia maintained order during an 1834 election riot in Philadelphia, an 1835 riot against the banks in Baltimore, an 1837 riot over the increasing cost of flour during a depression in New York City, helped to suppress the Nat Turner slave rebellion in Virginia in 1831, stopped a race riot in Providence, Rhode Island the same year, and in 1835 protected the lives and property of abolitionists during anti-abolitionist riots in New York City.

CONCLUSION

Thus, the anniversary decade of the 1830s marked the continued growth of the volunteer militia. Organized by diverse groups for social as well as military purposes, those often handsomely-clad community organizations served their cities, their states, and their country during the events of almost a century and a half ago.

— Martin K. Gordon

1836: THE GUARD'S TWO HUNDREDTH YEAR

BIBLIOGRAPHY

Gordon, Lawrence L., Maj. *Military Origins*. New York: A. S. Barnes & Co., 1971.

Headley, Joel T. *The Great Riots of New York: 1712-1873*. New York: E. B. Treat, 1873. Reprinted Indianapolis: The Bobbs-Merrill Company, Inc., 1970.

Hofstadter, Richard, and Wallace, Michael. *American Violence: A Documentary History*. New York: Vintage Books, 1971.

Love, Edmund G. "Officers of the 105th Infantry Regiment (27th Infantry Division) on Saipan, June 1944." *Military Collector & Historian* 2 (March 1950): 21-23.

Discusses the Troy, New York, National Guard on Saipan.

McBarron, H. Charles, Jr. "Troy Citizens Corps, 1836-1847." *Military Collector & Historian* 3 (March 1951): 18-19.

McConnell, Roland C. *Negro Troops of Antebellum Louisiana: A History of the Battalion of Free Men of Color*. Baton Rouge: Louisiana State Univ. Press, 1968.

Reinders, Robert. "Militia and Public Order in Nineteenth-Century America." *Journal of American Studies* 2 (April 1977): 81-101.

Smith, Paul T. "Militia of the United States from 1846 to 1860." *Indiana Magazine of History* 15 (1919): 20-47.

U. S. Army. Center of Military History. Organizational History Branch, "Unit Files: 210th Armor."

Weigley, Russell. *History of the United States Army*. The Macmillan Wars of the United States Series. New York: Macmillian, 1967.

For the Gaines call-up of the militia.

Wilson, Frederick T. *Federal Aid in Domestic Disturbances, 1787-1922*. New York: Arno Press Reprint of 1922 ed., 1969.

This essay has never been published before.

Part One
The Soldiers of August

August 1675 and August 1676 were important months for the militia in both the Northern and Southern colonies. In the North, King Philip's War flared and ended. On 2 August 1675 in the Upper Connecticut Valley, Captain Edward Hutchinson, some local citizens and friendly Indians, and twenty mounted militia lead by Captain Thomas Wheeler were ambushed outside of Brookfield, on their way to a parley with the local Nipmuck Indian tribe. Caught in a narrow defile, the party took heavy casualties and had to retreat to Brookfield. After a relieving force broke the ensuing Indian seige, the English colonists abandoned the town as being in an untenable location. The war continued. In the summer of 1676, a force of over 900 local soldiers from Massachusetts Bay, Connecticut, and Plymouth Colony, along with approximately 150 friendly Indians, took the field against King Philip and his supporters. That August saw the final pursuit and assault against the hostile Indians. On 12 August, a mixed force of experienced militia and friendly Indians caught King Philip at his home, outside the Narrangansett area. As the assault element pushed the surprised hostiles into the waiting blocking force, a friendly Indian killed the enemy leader after the musket of the Indian's white partner failed to fire.

In Virginia, August 1675, Indian raiders were increasing their attacks on the English settlers. The various local militias in the threatened areas staged reprisals, but were becoming frustrated with the colonial governor's policy of reconciliation towards the Indians. In early August 1676, because of this and other irritations, Nathaniel Bacon issued his "Declaration of the People." Basing his strength in the frontier militia, he began his revolt against the established coastal-oriented colonial authorities. Later, after much bitter fighting including the burning of Jamestown, Bacon and his military dictatorship was suppressed by loyal militia.

Racing ahead to the American Revolution, probably one of the most important contributions of the militia to the patriot cause took place 16 August 1777. Earlier, however, Brigadier General Nicholas Herkimer, on 6 August had led his force of 800 New York militia and Indians into an ambush outside of Oriskany, New York, while attempting to stop St. Leger's expedition from dividing the Northern colonies. Meanwhile, Burgoyne was continuing his advance that same August from Canada towards Albany, New York, with the identical goal of splitting the Rebel colonies. Poor planning and an over-optimistic hope for Loyalist support left the British and German force without adequate supplies. Burgoyne was forced to send a raiding party composed of predominately professional German mercenaries towards Bennington, Vermont, in the hope of obtaining horses, carriages, supplies and, in general, more Loyalist support.

Vermont and New Hampshire, becoming increasingly aroused over the conduct of the invaders, mobilized their militias. An experienced veteran of Bunker Hill, John Stark was commissioned brigadier general and given command of the New Hampshire state forces. Stark had resigned from the Continental Army that March after he had been passed over for promotion. Stark accepted his state commission and refused to take orders from the Continental Army's Major General Benjamin Lincoln because he was a state officer thus not responsible to the Continental authorities. Lincoln was able to work with Stark as an ally, though not as a subordinate.

On 8 August Stark moved his New Hampshiremen towards Bennington, to harrass Burgoyne's flank in cooperation with the Vermont militia and the Continental Army. Burgoyne sent 550 men towards Bennington the next day. Stark learned of the enemy movements on 13 August and called for reinforcements. The commander of the raiding party did likewise the next morning and he shortly thereafter formed his men into defensive positions. Stark attacked with skirmishers on the 15th. On the 16th, his New Hampshire and Vermont forces attacked in strength. The component units of the German, British, and allied forces reacted in different ways. Some ran early in the battle while other units fought until they had sustained heavy

The Battle of Bennington as portrayed by Alonzo Chappel. General John Stark, commander of the New Hampshire state army is on horseback in the right center directing his men. Note the casually clad militiamen in the left foreground leading off their Hessian prisoners. The battle took place 16 August 1777.

casualties and were out of ammunition. Stark's men carried the first battle of that day. As it was ending, the German reinforcements arrived at the site about the same time as Continental and Vermont reinforcements arrived for Stark. A second battle ensued which Stark and his men also won. The two battles of Bennington that August day cost Burgoyne approximately 900 men as well as the much-needed supplies. It also gave American morale a needed boost. After more sharp conflicts, Burgoyne surrendered 17 October 1777.

The most recent 200 years of militia happenings in August will be reported in next month's "The Soldiers of August: Part II."

—Martin K. Gordon

THE SOLDIERS OF AUGUST: PART ONE

BIBLIOGRAPHY

Boatner, Mark M. Encyclopedia of the American Revolution. New York: David McKay Co., Inc., 1966.

Carson, Jane. Bacon's Rebellion, 1676-1976. Jamestown, VA: The Jamestown Foundation, 1976.

Dictionary of American Biography, vol 17. "Stark, John." by Edward E. Curtis.

Leach, Douglas E. Flintlock and Tomahawk: New England in King Philip's War. New York: The Macmillan Co., 1958.

Morison, Samuel Eliot. The Oxford History of the American People. New York: Oxford Univ. Press, 1965.

For King Philip's War.

Peckham, Howard H., ed. The Toll of Independence: Engagements and Battle Casualties of the American Revolution. Chicago: The Univ. of Chicago Press, 1974.

ERRATUM

The illustration is from the Dover Pictorial Archives.

This essay originally appeared in the July 1977 Push Pin Post.

THE SOLDIERS OF AUGUST: PART II

Henry Francis Du Pont Winterthur Museum

Kemmelmeyer's painting shows Washington at Fort Cumberland, Virginia, reviewing some of the 12,950 militia called out to suppress the Whiskey Rebellion in Pennsylvania. Washington's use of this militia army set a precedent followed by President Eisenhower at Little Rock, Arkansas, in 1957 and President Kennedy at Oxford, Mississippi, in 1962.

As we saw last month, August is a meaningful month for the militia. After a long forced march on 19 August 1779, Major Henry ("Light-Horse Harry") Lee led about 400 Virginia and Maryland cavalry and infantry in a surprise attack on the British outpost at Paulus Hook (in modern Jersey City), New Jersey. At a cost of 11 casualties, the militia killed about 50 and captured 158 enemy soldiers. Loyalist militia under Lieutenant Colonel Abraham Van Buskirk attacked them on their way back from the victory that day. British regulars also tried to stop them. The revolutionary forces lost three captured in those skirmishes. That August action cost the British their last post in New Jersey.

August 1794 marked an important milestone for the peacetime militia. George Washington, in that month, established a precedent which endures with modifications to this day. Confronted with the first major threat against the new government, he turned to an early version of the federalized Guard to uphold the U.S. Constitution rather than to the regular armed forces. He did not believe that regulars should be used against American citizens. For a variety of reasons centered around the federal excise tax on distilled spirits, the western counties of Pennsylvania had begun rioting against the civil authorities. Supreme Court Justice James Wilson, 4 August, triggered the militia call-up system when he formally notified President Washington that the demonstrations were beyond the control of the civil authorities. Washington, 7 August, set the pattern when he asked Pennsylvania, New Jersey, Maryland, and Virginia, for an immediate mobilization of 12,950 militia. As the militia was mobilized, the governors of Pennsylvania, New Jersey, and Virginia took the field as commanders of their state's forces. Washington, as commander in chief appointed the same Light-Horse Harry Lee, now governor of Virginia, as field commander of the "Army of the Constitution" as it was known. The rioteers dispersed in the face of that large disciplined militia force and order was restored without the use of the regular Army.

August 1814 saw the literal high-water mark of the British assaults on the Eastern seaboard of the United States during the War of 1812. On 20 August 1814, the 4,500 soldiers and sailors of a British raiding party were encamped 45 miles from Washington, D.C. Tuesday, 23 August two regiments of Baltimore militia occupied a strong defensive position against the British. They were relocated to a weaker position before the battle started. Washington, Annapolis, and elements of the Virginia militia were also called out. On 24 August the clash came at Bladensburg, Maryland. While still fighting, the third line of militia was ordered to retreat by the Army general commanding the American forces at the battle. Denied permission to stand and fight, the militia of that line of resistance melted away when they were ordered to retreat past their homes in the District of Columbia. The British were able to temporarily occupy the capital city during that August of 1814.

August 1824 is a very special month in the history of the militia. That was the month when the 2d Battalion, 11th Regiment, New York Artillery, which later became the 7th Regiment of New York, adopted the name National Guards in honor of the Marquis de Lafayett's old French command. From that beginning, came the present designation of National Guard for the organized citizen-soldiery of the United States.

The enthusiasm of the New York City militiamen for the Marquis and his famous unit also helped solve a political problem facing the officers and men of the 2d Battalion. They had wanted to organize a new battalion with a new name but had been unable to agree upon the name. They had considered several names such as the "New York City Guard," the "Washington Guards," and the "Independence Battalion," without accepting any of them. In the middle of August, while these discussions were going on and on, the Marquis de Lafayette arrived in New York City. He arrived in New York on 16 August. On 25 August 1824, the officers organizing the new battalion voted, "Resolved, That the Battalion of Infantry attached to the Eleventh Regiment, N.Y.S. Artillery, be hereafter known and distinguished by the name of National Guards."

The Augusts of the first 50 years of the United States saw many important happenings in the life of the National Guard. Among them, President George Washington determined their proper role in upholding the Constitution in August, and, in a later August, the term National Guards, later changed to singular, entered the vocabulary of the American people and its part-time soldiers.

—Martin K. Gordon

THE SOLDIERS OF AUGUST: PART II

BIBLIOGRAPHY

THE AMERICAN REVOLUTION

Boatner, Mark M. Encyclopedia of the American Revolution. New York: David McKay Co., 1966.

Coakley, Robert W., and Conn, Stetson. The War of the American Revolution: Narrative, Chronology, and Bibliography. A Bicentennial Publication of the United States Army Center of Military History. Washington: Government Printing Office, 1975.

Lee, Henry "Light Horse Harry." The American Revolution in the South. Edited by Robert E. Lee. New York: Arno Press, 1969 reprint of Memoirs of the War in the Southern Department of the United States. New York: University Publishing Co., 1869.

Peckham, Howard H., ed. The Toll of Independence: Engagements and Battle Casualties of the American Revolution.

THE WHISKEY REBELLION

Gordon, Martin K. "The District of Columbia Militia, 1790-1815." Ph. D. dissertation, The George Washington University, 1975.

THE WAR OF 1812

Gordon, Martin K. Cited above.

Mahon, John K. The War of 1812. Gainesville: University of Florida Press, 1972.

1824

Clark, Emmons, Col., History of the Seventh Regiment of New York, 1806-1889. New York: Pub. by the Seventh Regiment, 1890. 2 vols.

ERRATUM

The U. S. Army Center of Military History considers the attack on Paulus Hook to be an all-Continental Army operation.

This essay was originally published in the August 1977 Push Pin Post.

The Soldiers of August: The Civil War

Manassas, Virginia, August 30, 1862, the defeat of the army under General Pope on the battlefield of 1st Manassas (Bull Run).

August 1862 marked one of those bloody battles of the Civil War which opened the way to a new phase of that conflict. The Civil War became serious with a battle hard fought at Bull Run as the Union called it, or Manassas Junction as it was known to the Confederacy in July 1861. The site was of great strategic importance as it marked the intersection of one of the main roads to Richmond with a railroad net that led not only west to the Shenandoah Valley but more importantly south to the new Confederate capital of Richmond. That combination of railroads and surface roads assured an overland approach for the Union armies that avoided many of the natural barriers that would have to be overcome along the shortest route. A few miles east of the Bull Run Mountains of Virginia, the intersection was approximately 25 miles southwest of Washington, D.C.

The July 1861 conflict between the two armies of eager but untrained regulars and militiamen ended with the Confederacy in control of that northernmost of its defensive areas. It later retreated south and the Union army established a supply depot there. August 28–30, 1862 marked a second Union defeat at the same place that paved the way for Robert E. Lee's first invasion of the North.

Lincoln gave Major General John Pope command of the newly created Army of Virginia in June. His missions were to defend Washington, D.C., and the Shenandoah Valley, while acting aggressively against the Confederates north of Richmond so that pressure would be drawn away from Major General George B. McClellan's attack against the Confederate capital from the southeast. McClellan was forced to withdraw, and Lee turned his attention to Pope and his 47,000 officers and men, hoping to force him to withdraw from the interior of Virginia before McClellan could come around Virginia and reinforce Pope. Through reinforcing "Stonewall" Jackson and his famous "foot cavalry" that once marched approximately 51 miles in two days, Lee was able to outfight, and with Jackson's flanking actions, force Pope to withdraw. Jackson, on August 25, sent J.E.B. Stuart and his cavalry in a sweep around Pope to capture his base of supplies at Manassas Junction. That was easily accomplished. Jackson then joined Stuart and they then destroyed what of Pope's supplies they could not eat, drink, or carry off.

Pope, on August 27th learned of Jackson's actions and immediately ordered his army to concentrate on Manassas. He believed that he had Jackson trapped and began to issue victory announcements. Unfortunately, he did not realize that he was marching into a trap Lee had set for him. The bait for the trap was set the next day when Jackson's infantry attacked a volunteer brigade of Wisconsin and Indiana regiments on the road on their way to where they had been told the battle would be fought. The brigade commander sent the 2nd Wisconsin and 19th Indiana to chase away the ambushers. Then the mass of Confederate infantry appeared in the field. The 6th and 7th Wisconsin were sent in.

Two more brand-new militia regiments, the 56th Pennsylvania and the 76th New York, were thrown into the fray.

Jackson had developed a line behind good defensive terrain. Pope sent his men marching and countermarching in several directions to try to locate Jackson. Meanwhile Pope kept announcing his victory. The main battle took place August 29–30. On the 29th, Pope sent his German volunteers, under Major General Franz Sigel, against Jackson. Other volunteer regiments in that assault were composed of Michigan, Pennsylvania, and New York volunteer units as well as regulars. Pope thought his men had won the battle that day although they had only gained, not held, parts of Jackson's position. Pope then ordered Major General Fitz-John Porter to take his corps and outflank Jackson. Porter, carrying out his orders, suddenly discovered Confederate Major General James Longstreet and his 30,000 veteran soldiers in front of him—where they had advanced completely undetected.

Pope ordered a pursuit the next morning, August 30th. He refused to believe that the Confederate skirmish lines were anything more than a rear guard. Fortunately, Porter, although joining in the attack, had pulled the 5th and 10th New York out of line and with a battery of regular artillery, sent them to guard his flank during the battle. The rebels suddenly counterattacked on the front and attacked on the flank. The Union army fell back. The Confederate advance on the flank rolled right over the 10th New York, but the 5th New York, a Zouave regiment, held long enough for the artillery to get away. The regiment lost 347 killed or wounded out of 490 men present that day. The 12th Massachusetts and other regiments slugged it out with Hood's Texas Brigade which now joined in the fray. The Union army retreated, usually in good order. Regular and volunteer alike, it was now a veteran force that did not break and run.

—Martin K. Gordon

THE SOLDIERS OF AUGUST: THE CIVIL WAR

BIBLIOGRAPHY

Catton, Bruce. *The Army of the Potomac. Vol 1: Mr. Lincoln's Army*. Garden City: Doubleday & Co., 1962.

Dictionary of American Biography, vol. 11. "Longstreet, James." by Douglas Southall Freeman.

Jones, Virgil C. "First Manassas: The Story of the Bull Run Campaign." *Civil War Times Illustrated* (1973): 1-50.

    A special issue.

Wilshin, Francis F. *Manassas (Bull Run) National Battlefield Park Virginia*. National Park Service Historical Handbook Series No. 15. Washington: Government Printing Office, 1953.

This essay originally appeared in the August 1978 *Push Pin Post*.

The Soldiers of August: The Transition to Today's Guard

August 20, 1866, President Andrew Johnson declared the Civil War to be officially over. Earlier, on April 2, President Johnson had proclaimed the insurrection at an end in all states except Texas. But that August end of the Civil War in Texas enabled the President to proclaim, "peace, order, tranquility, and civil authority now exist in and throughout the whole of the United States." An estimated 1,933,779 militia or National Guardsmen, black and white had served on active duty for varying lengths of time during that war.

The National Guard, as it came to be called during and after the Civil War, was actively involved in maintaining law and order as American society made the rough transition from an agricultural to an industrial way of life. August 1878, when Illinois called out a National Guard company to disperse rioting miners and guard a local jail, or August 1884, when Louisiana called out between 200 and 300 Guardsmen to recover a courthouse from an armed mob, or when Alabama twice in August 1888 called out National Guard companies to control mobs, all mark occasions when state authorities relied on the citizen-soldiers to maintain order.

THE NEW MOOD

These years between the Civil War and the Spanish-American War also marked the beginnings of the modern Guard oriented towards both a state and a federal mission. Regular Army officers were occasionally detailed to the states for training or inspector assignments and marksmanship became a major emphasis in Guard training. Although the Guard did not lose its social flavor, an August 1877 declaration by New York's *National Guardsman*, a weekly that began publication that August, caught the new moods of professionalism and enthusiasm:

We believe in the National Guard—in its Divine authentication, its present purpose, and the glorious possibilities of its future . . .
We believe in Rifle Practice as an important element of National Guard education—its benefits in promoting manliness, healthfulness, self-reliance, coolness, nerve and skill . . .
We believe in efficiency on the part of the commissioned officers—that the day has gone by when good-fellowship, a plethoric pocketbook, or political influence could command a commission.
We believe in the moral influence for good of the Citizen-Soldier—that the armory and the parade ground . . . comprehend schools wherein the members of the National Guard may learn their duty to God and man.

THE SPANISH-AMERICAN WAR AND ITS AFTERMATH

The first test of this new outlook came during and after the Spanish-American War of April–August 1898. Although the National Guard was promptly mustered into Federal service for this war, few of the units reached the combat zones before the Spanish surrender. One exception was the Puerto Rican campaign begun July 21, 1898. Artillery from Pennsylvania, infantry from Massachusetts, Illinois, and Wisconsin along with cavalry from New York were included in the attacking force, to name but a few of the participating states. The experience of Troop C, New York Volunteer Cavalry was not untypical. (Then a Brooklyn, New York unit, this troop is now perpetuated by the 101st Cavalry of Staten Island and the Finger Lakes District of New York.)

Captain Bertram T. Clayton, a New York Congressman and captain in Troop C, referred to the air between the decks of the Troop's transport as being, "like sewer gas." The ship ran aground and by the time Troop C arrived at its bivouac area, the Philadelphia First City Troop had already taken the shady part of the new camp ground next to a church. The conquest of Puerto Rico took place that August. All combat arms were involved in the conquest of Coamo where the Spanish chose to stand and fight. As the end of the war seemed close, Spanish resistance became light elsewhere and the Guardsmen and regulars had no difficulty in taking their assigned objectives. The 4th Ohio Infantry, for example, which had arrived in Puerto Rico on August 1, suffered the only casualties, one officer and four enlisted wounded, during the seizure of Guayama from 400 Spaniards. The Spanish regular and volunteer forces signed an armistice on August 13, 1898.

In the Philippine campaign, the 10th Pennsylvania Volunteer Infantry, supported by Utah and regular artillery and with the 1st California Volunteers in reserve, was the first American unit to come under enemy fire on Philippine soil. It happened the night of July 31–August 1 when the Spanish began heavy firing into the American trenches. The Americans lost ten killed and 43 wounded without even seeing the Spanish that night. Volunteer state forces continued to fight in the Philippines after the Spanish surrender, against Filipino insurrectionists who wanted immediate independence for that country.

—Martin K. Gordon

Troop C, New York Volunteer Cavalry, now the 101st Cavalry, NYNG, on the way to Guayama, Puerto Rico during the Spanish-American War. (Photo courtesty of the National Archives)

THE SOLDIERS OF AUGUST:

THE TRANSITION TO TODAY'S GUARD

BIBLIOGRAPHY

Derthick, Martha. The National Guard in Politics. Cambridge: Harvard Univ. Press, 1965.

Freidel, Frank. The Splendid Little War. New York: Bramhall House, n.d.

Trussell, John B. B., ed., "A Pennsylvanian in the Philippines: Extracts from the Letters of Corporal William S. Christner, 1898-1899." Pennsylvania History 44 (April 1977): 117-149.

U. S. Army. Center of Military History. Organizational History Branch. "Unit Files: 101st Cavalry."

U. S. Congress. House of Representatives. Committee on the Militia. Efficiency of the Militia. H. R. Rept. 754, 52d Cong., 1st sess., 1892.

U. S. National Guard Bureau. The National Guard in America's Wars. Fact Sheet Number 105-75. Washington: National Guard Bureau, July, 1975.

This essay originally appeared in the August 1979 Push Pin Post.

300 Years of the National Guard

1676

It was almost 70 years since the first Jamestown landings, and the United States was only a glint in the eye of history when the tradition of the citizen-soldier began in North America.

Forty years after the establishment of the first unit of the organized militia and one hundred years before the great War for American Independence, militiamen were engaged in major conflicts across the colonies. In New England, a force of over 900 local soldiers from Massachusetts Bay, Connecticut, and Plymouth Colony, along with approximately 150 friendly Indians, were fighting in what was known as King Philip's War against the strongholds of the Wampanoag Indians. 1676 was the second year of that war. In April, Canonchet, one of the abler remaining Indian leaders, was ambushed and captured. That August King Philip himself was captured and killed. The war slowly ground to a halt.

Meanwhile, further south, rebellion broke out against the authority of the colonial governor in Virginia. 1676 was the second and final year of Nathaniel Bacon's revolt. He had turned frontier frustrations with the falling price of tobacco, the politicking of the royal governor, and an official policy of reconciliation towards the sometime unfriendly Indians, into a full-scaled rebellion. He marched into Jamestown, the colonial capital, 23 June 1676 with 400 infantry and 120 cavalry and forced the governor to flee to the loyal areas along the coast. Making his last stand ironically near Yorktown, the site of the British and Loyalist defeat a little over 100 years later, he died there and the rebellion was broken by loyal militia before regular troops could arrive from England.

1776

The American Revolution raged and General George Washington was just raising his Continental Army. Many militia units were absorbed into Washington's new army. Their story is well-known. But other militia units continued to serve in what might be called "state" status.

In Philadelphia, John Ross, an upholsterer by trade, was on patrol duty January 21, 1776 with his unit of the Philadelphia Associators, a volunteer militia organization. While walking his guard post along the Philadelphia docks, he was killed by the accidental explosion of a quantity of gunpowder stored nearby. His widow, Mrs. Betsy Ross, carried on his business and, in addition, made flags for the Pennsylvania and Continental forces. The Associators stayed on active duty throughout George Washington's Trenton-Princeton campaign of 1776-1777, serving both as home guard and as offensive forces. The Dover Light Infantry Company of the Kent County, Delaware militia had also mobilized that winter. In the one month of its active duty it participated in that important campaign which was to reverse the defeats of earlier that year.

The militia also rallied in defense of their homes against British raiders. Militia from Bristol and Warren, Rhode Island, January 12-14, 1776, fought British naval raiding parties, in one case on Prudence Island in Nar-

ragansett Bay engaging in a three-hour fire fight. On January 20th in New York, General Philip Schuyler leading 3000 militiamen forced Sir John Johnson of Johnstown, New York, and 700 other Loyalists to surrender, thereby breaking the back of loyalist resistance in the Albany area and assuring the neutrality of neighboring Indians for some time to come.

Elsewhere, the Maryland militia serving at Norfolk, Virginia drove HMS *Otter* and two tenders away from American schooners. Colonel Richard Caswell with 1000 militiamen routed Colonel Donald McLeod and 1200 Loyalists at Moore's Creek Bridge, Cape Fear River, North Carolina.

1876

One hundred years old and still growing, that was America in 1876. The militia would soon become the National Guard, but the tradition wouldn't change.

In 1876, the centennial year of the United States, organized volunteer militia units were active in three areas of service.

At the Centennial Fair in Philadelphia, volunteer units armed with sabers and bayonets helped the badly outnumbered police maintain order at the opening day ceremonies May 10, 1876. There was barely enough room for President Grant and his party to take their places at the ceremonies. The press and other invited guests could not always find their seats because of the opening day crowds. Thus the militia played a major role in helping insure the success of the day. Later on in the summer, of course, those units, not only from Philadelphia, but also from other parts of the country, participated in the ceremonial aspects of the nation's centennial.

Another aspect of the militia's 1876 service was demonstrated in Tennessee. That January, a detachment of the state militia was called up to fight hostile Indians.

Order was also important that election year throughout the South, as Reconstruction drew to a close. Black and white militia units sometimes maintained order and

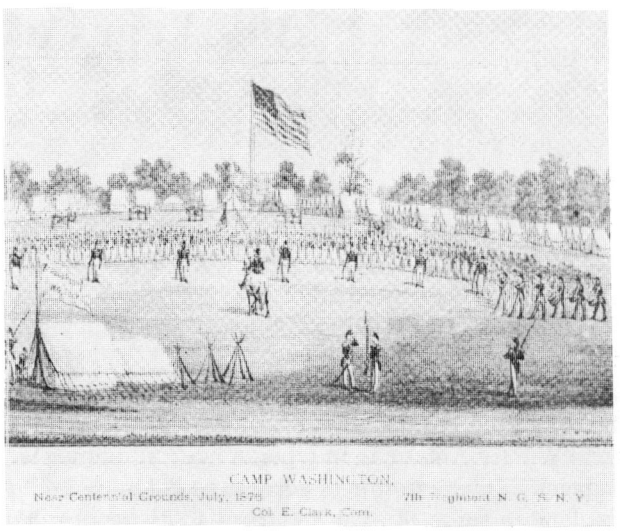

sometimes violated it as the most important presidential election since the end of the Civil War heated up. As a foreshadowing of some of the militia's most time-consuming work of the remainder of that decade, one regiment of the New Jersey militia was called up that October to protect property and quell an anticipated railroad workers riot.

1976

It is our time, and the nation's bicentennial is upon us. Muskets, smooth-bore cannon and pack horses are gone, replaced by M-16s, self-propelled howitzers and jet planes. The world of today's citizen-soldier is very different from that of his great-grandfather, or grandfather, or father, but the tradition and heritage remain, a living tribute to the will of men and women to place and keep their defense in their own hands.

Our militia heritage, not many of us keep these roots in mind as we go about our day to day business. But the strength of the Army and Air National Guard rests on a tradition of service that goes back well over 300 years and technical expertise and job proficiency in the world of the modern Army and Air Force.

We have come full cycle. During the colonial and early national periods of United States history, the militia was the solid (and sometimes not so solid) core of American defense. During the late nineteenth century and through the early twentieth century, the active military establishment expanded dramatically. Now, the "Total Force Policy" brings American military policy back to its roots — dependence upon the citizen-soldier.

The Air Force has been considerably ahead of the other services in its support and integration of the reserve with the active forces. We are rightfully proud of this fact. Now new missions and new capabilities have come to the Guard. Ski-equipped C-130's, KC-135 Jet Tankers, HC-130's and HH-3's (the latter part of the aerospace recovery team) are just a few of the new aircraft and missions coming to the Air Guard.

The Army National Guard is rapidly being integrated into the active Army. Four Guard brigades for all intents and purposes "round out" active Divisions and, of course, our eight Divisions are considered part of the Army's 24 Division force. Many other ARNG units are affiliated with or are involved in direct mutual support of active Army units. The Guard is also receiving new equipment, like the M48A5 tank and the modernized M109 self-propelled howitzer. Guard units are also slated to receive new communications equipment in the future, an area of great weakness in the reserve forces in general.

The citizen-soldier, an enduring figure in American military efforts. A tradition in American life that has an exciting future.

Paris, France. American troops of the 28th Infantry Division march down the Champs Elysees in the "Victory parade," 1945. (Photo by Poinsett)

300 YEARS OF THE NATIONAL GUARD

BIBLIOGRAPHY

1676

Carson, Jane. Bacon's Rebellion, 1676-1976. Jamestown, VA: The Jamestown Foundation, 1976.

Leach, Douglas E. Arms for Empire: A Military History of the British Colonies in North America, 1607-1763. The Macmillan Wars of the United States Series. New York: The Macmillan Company, 1971.

_____. Flintlock and Tomahawk: New England in King Philip's War. New York: The Macmillan Company, 1958.

Peckham, Howard H. The Colonial Wars, 1689-1762. The Chicago History of American Civilization Series. Chicago: Univ. of Chicago Press, 1964.

Washburn, Wilcomb E. The Governor and the Rebel: A History of Bacon's Rebellion in Virginia. New York: W.W. Norton & Co., 1972.

1776

Coakley, Robert W., and Conn, Stetson. The War of the American Revolution: Narrative, Chronology, and Bibliography. A Bicentennial Publication of the United States Army Center of Military History. Washington: Government Printing Office, 1975.

Trussell, John B.B., Jr. Pennsylvania Landmarks of the Revolution. N.p.: Pub. by Bicentennial Commission of Pennsylvania, 1976?

1876

Brown, Dee. The Year of the Century: 1876. New York: Charles Scribner's Sons, 1966.

U. S. Congress. House of Representatives. Committee on the Militia. Efficiency of the Militia. H. R. Rept. 754, 52d Cong., 1st sess., 1892.

ERRATUM

In the last paragraph of 1776 essay, Continental, Virginia, and perhaps North Carolina soldiers participated in the action at Norfolk, Virginia, not Maryland troops.

This essay was first published in the July 1976 Push Pin Post.

Preaching at the militia

By Martin K. Gordon

Chaplains have been accompanying militia into action at least since 1637. Samuel Stone of Hartford, Connecticut was a settled civilian pastor selected officially to accompany Captain John Mason and his force against the Pequot Indians as a chaplain that year. Likewise, civilian pastor John Wilson of Boston was chosen to accompany the Massachusetts forces in the field that summer to minister to their spiritual needs. Specially chosen clergy have been included in mobilizations from colonial times to the present.

The flavor of those exhortations to obey God and the legal authorities of the colony has been captured in the title of the artillery election sermon Urian Oakes preached in Boston June 3, 1672, "The unconquerable, all-conquering, and more than conquering souldier: or the successful warre which a believer wageth with the enemies of his soul: as also the absolute and unparalleled victory that he obtains finally over them into the Ancient and Honorable Artillery Company of Massachusetts.

This 1867 painting, "Pilgrims Going To Church", serves as a reminder of the close ties between the colonial citizen-soldiers and their clergy. The original is in the New York Historical Society. (Photo courtesy of the Library of Congress)

I Peace Time Roles

Forgotten by most, however, was the peacetime role of the pastors who spoke to the militiamen on their spring training days and on the occasion of their election of officers. These training-day, or artillery election sermons as they are called, also contributed to the early development of a strong militia system. This custom of the sermon was widespread in New England, but the term artillery election sermon has clung to them because of the large surviving group that were preached to the artillery company of Boston. That unit has since evolved through the love of God in Jesus Christ. . . ."

The clergy compared their soldiers with David going forth to fight Goliath who in that context could be translated into either the Indians, French, Spanish, pirates, or just a general exhortation to readiness as the case may be. The sermons were usually preached early in the summer or in late spring at the beginning of the muster season. Those reminders to duty must have reinforced the importance of militia drill as well as the concept of civilian supremacy in the minds of the listeners.

II A Sample Sermon

"Zechariah's vision of Christ's Martial Glory" was preached June 3, 1728. The anonymous author told the militia God sent the various offices and colors, "for soldiers to know their leaders and keep Rank and Order." The angels in scripture were termed "in a martial character, for they are here represented in a war-like character formed into a strong Battalion . . . They are good soldiers of Jesus Christ under his command . . . The Captain of our salvation is Captain-General of the heavenly hosts . . . From what hath been said, Those of the Military Order may be exhorted and incited to the duties of their station."

"By viewing the Angelick Artillery, the Celestial Cavalcade, which the vision exhibits to us, Soldiers may learn what they ought to do, and be excited to the faithful discharge of all that is incumbent on them." They were told to obey their commander in all things "and be ready to attend whenever he shall order your appearance in the Field of Battle." They were reminded to fight valiantly because not only magistrates and ministers but also soldiers were appointed to guard and defend the church. "To be led into the Field by a victorious General, and with valiant soldiers may well animate the greatest coward to fight. Courage is a necessary qualification of a Soldier; the greatest Skill and Strength without it, are of little use in war. The Exercise of it is difficult when a man looks a potent Enemy in the Face, and marcheth into the Mouth of Danger, heareth the roaring Cannons and Guns, and the confused horrible noise with which every Battle of the Warrior is attended."

III Conclusion

After warnings like that preached at the start of every season throughout the muster fields of New England, soldiers certainly had a lot to think about. Those sermons explained the meaning and importance of the annual musters. Inspections of weapons and equipment, drills in the sun, and eligibility for call-up in time of need, as well as a chance to spend the day with one's neighbors in a picnic setting, here became the reminders of the serious side of being a citizen-soldier in the New World.

PREACHING AT THE MILITIA

BIBLIOGRAPHY

DISCUSSIONS OF THE SERMONS

Ahearn, Marie L. "David, the Military Exemplum." In The David Myth in Western Literature, pp. 106-119, 200-202. Edited by Raymond-Jean Frontain and Jan Wojcik. West Lafayette, IN: Purdue Univ. Press, 1980.

Concise analysis of the use of the King David the warrior symbol in colonial militia sermons to promote support for a godly militia and just warfare.

Boorstin, Daniel J. The Americans: The Colonial Experience. Middlesex, England: Pelican Books, 1963.

Higginbotham, Don. The War of American Independence: Military Attitudes, Policies, and Practice, 1763-1789. The Macmillan Wars of the United States Series. New York: The Macmillan Company, 1971.

Honeywell, Ray J. Chaplains of the United States Army. Washington, DC: Office of the Chief of Chaplains, U. S. Army, 1958.

Leach, Douglas E. Arms for Empire: A Military History of the British Colonies in North America, 1607-1763. The Macmillan Wars of the United States Series. New York: The Macmillan Company, 1971.

Plumstead, A. W. comp. The Wall and the Garden: Selected Massachusetts Election Sermons, 1670-1775. Minneapolis: Univ. of Minnesota Press, 1968.

THE SERMONS

The sermons cited in the essay are part of a large collection of "election" and "training day" sermons maintained in the Rare Books and Special Collections Division of The Library of Congress.

ERRATUM

The credit line for the illustration should read simply courtesy of the New-York Historical Society.

This essay originally appeared in the April 1979 Push Pin Post.

John Philip Sousa: Martial Music for the Militia

John Philip Sousa, "the march king," is usually associated with the band of the United States Marine Corps. Yet he spent most of his career leading his own band and served with the United States Navy in World War I. He also wrote six marches between 1873 and 1924 for various militia/National Guard units.

Very little is known about Sousa's first published march, "Review," written in the summer of 1873, except that it was dedicated to Colonel William G. Moore of the Washington, D.C. Light Infantry. Perhaps this unit had an influence on Sousa since he was only 20 at the time he wrote it and had grown up in Washington.

Indeed, four of Sousa's six marches were dedicated to and written for District of Columbia militia units, reflecting his interest in the city where he had not only grown up, but also was stationed with the Marine Band. His 1888 "National Fencibles" was intended for use as the "march past" of a unit by that name, and included these words which reflect the martial esprit of the times: "Forward to battle, the trumpet is sounding; 'Come if you dare!' We loudly sing. Shoulder to shoulder, with hearts rebounding; Onward we march with the Fencibles' swing." Jealous, the cadets of the militia corps at Washington's high school asked Sousa in 1890 if he would write a superior march for their use. He complied with 'The High School Cadets,'' which became one of Sousa's more popular marches. The cadets liked the march and after they heard it at a Marine Band rehearsal, they contributed 24 dollars to have the march published and copyrighted.

The same year he wrote the "Corcoran Cadets" for a company by that name. This unit was named after a locally prominent business-

John Philip Sousa and his band at the 1893 Exposition in St. Louis, Missouri courtesy of the U.S. Marine Corps.

man, William W. Corcoran, probably in the hope of raising money from him. Corcoran also had offered to contribute towards Sousa's music training at one time so this militia march also gave Sousa the opportunity to show his gratitude. These two 1890 marches were among the first Sousa compositions to be recorded for the new phonograph.

Sousa resigned from the Marine Band in 1892 to form his own concert band. Although it was not a marching band, the Sousa Band was known to have marched in seven parades in the 39 years of its existence. Two of those occasions were with National Guard units. The band was in Cleveland on the morning of May 5, 1898 when Troop A, originally known as the First City Troop and later the Black Horse Squadron, of the Ohio National Guard was marching to the train depot to participate in the Spanish-American War. The band joined the parade and escorted the Troop to the station. Sousa previously marched with the Troop in 1881 when, as leader of the Marine Band, he and his men had marched with tha Guard unit in the funeral cortege of President James A. Garfield. In 1924, at the request of the unit, he wrote "The Black Horse Troop" and presented it in Cleveland, October 17, 1925 at a Sousa Band concert which also marked the 48th anniversary of Troop A.

The end of the Spanish-American War marked another of those rare occasions when the Sousa Band actually marched. On September 11, 1898, the band, then appearing in Pittsburgh, marched in a parade celebrating the return of the 18th Regiment, Pennsylvania volunteers from that war.

"The Gallant Seventh," the last of Sousa's militia marches, was in honor of the 7th Regiment, 107th Infantry, of the New York National Guard. Although other composers wrote marches for this famous regiment, Sousa's was the only one to gain wide acceptance. The 7th Regiment Band augmented the Sousa Band for the first performance of this march at the New York Hippodrome, November 5, 1922.

When John Philip Sousa died March 6, 1932 at Reading, Pennsylvania, it was only fitting that an honor guard from the Pennsylvania National Guard accompanied his remains back to Washington, D.C., for his funeral and burial.

Martin K. Gordon

JOHN PHILIP SOUSA: MARTIAL MUSIC FOR THE MILITIA

BIBLIOGRAPHY

Bierley, Paul E. *John Philip Sousa: A Descriptive Catalog of His Works*. Urbana: University of Illinois Press, 1973.

―――――. *John Philip Sousa: American Phenomenon*. Englewood Cliffs, NJ: Prentice-Hall, Inc., 1973.

The author acknowledges the assistance of Mr. Bierley with gratitude.

This essay originally appeared in the October 1976 *Push Pin Post*.

The Black Militia and the Revolution

One of the continually evolving themes in the history of the American military has been the question of participation of black soldiers in the national military effort. It was not until after the Civil War that permanent black militia units were permitted throughout the country. The integration of those units into the mainstream white Guard was not achieved until after World War II.

The question of the use of black soldiers had two perspectives in the American Revolution. At the national level, George Washington was concerned both with maintaining his own strength and with the denial of black manpower to the enemy British Army. The valor of black soldiers at the Battle of Bunker Hill and in other early battles combined with the British appeals to black men to come into their Army to influence both General Washington and the Continental Congress to allow black participation on the revolutionary side. In the southern colonies, efforts to encourage or force both slave and free blacks to remain on the revolutionary side and thus away from British influences were as much a consideration as was the positive need for manpower.

Early Integration

The foundations of this debate in North Carolina, for example, dates at least from 1715 when the colonial government decided not to arm slaves in the face of the threat of French and Spanish raids. Policy towards freed men varied between the colonies as in the 1750s when both blacks and mulattoes participated in North Carolina while at the same time, they were forbidden to participate in the Maryland militia.

Interestingly, as Jeffrey J. Crow points out for North Carolina, slaves were attracted towards British service because of the promise of freedom that was held out to them while freedmen, who pre-

A sketch of Continental soldiers made in 1781 by a French officer. (Photo courtesy of The Library of Congress)

An armed hunter as imagined by an artist of the 1880s. (Photo courtesy of the Library of Congress and Century Magazine)

sumably had a stake in society, tended to enlist in either American state or Continental service. Perhaps the most outstanding exemplars of that participation were the black citizen-soldiers who, as members of Colonel John Glover's Marblehead, Massachusetts regiment helped row George Washington and his men across the Delaware River to attack Trenton, New Jersey on December 25, 1777. The fishing industry in the home towns of those soldiers was integrated and when the regiment was reorganized for Revolutionary War service, both races volunteered and participated together. It is that seagoing background that also helps to explain black participation in the state and Continental navies.

Most black soldiers preferred to enlist in the Continental Army because of its longer tours which led to greater stability. But that does not mean that freedmen and slaves alike did not contribute to the local defense efforts. They served in local defense forces, mustering to meet specific threats, guarding stores, and contributing their labor to military construction projects. For example, in June 1781, Continental Army Major General Nathanael Greene ordered a subordinate, "to collect as may of the Militia and Negroes as you can and employ them in demolishing the works upon the Savannah River."

Revolutionary Uniforms

The question of what did the black militiaman look like in the American Revolution is a very difficult one. Militiamen in general were not as distinctively uniformed as they came to be after the War of 1812 twenty-eight years later. For example, at the Battle of Ramsour's Mill (near present-day Lincolnton, North Carolina) in June 1780, the revolutionary militia wore scraps of white paper in their hats while the Tories wore a spring of green leaves to distinguish themselves. Accounts of militiamen practically in rags continually appear. Questions of should Continental supplies be issued to short-term soldiers, the occasional refusal of a state legislature to authorize a clothes allowance, and, of course, wartime shortages, all contributed to what must have been a varied appearance. Thus the two illustrations used this month indicate the extremes of an armed black hunter and of a black soldier in, most likely, a Continental dress uniform. Somewhere within the extremes of those men lies the appearance of the black citizen-soldier as he contributed to both his country and his history.

——Martin K. Gordon

THE BLACK MILITIA AND THE REVOLUTION

BIBLIOGRAPHY

Crow, Jeffrey J.   The Black Experience in Revolutionary North Carolina. Raleigh: Dept. of Cultural Resources, 1977.

Quarles, Benjamin. "The Colonial Militia and Negro Manpower." Mississippi Valley Historical Review 45 (1959): 643-652.

_____.   The Negro in the American Revolution. New York: W. W. Norton & Co., Inc., 1973.

Rankin, Hugh. North Carolina in the American Revolution. Raleigh: Dept. of Cultural Resources, 1975.

This essay originally appeared in the February 1979 Push Pin Post.

The Battalion of Free Men of Color

Louisiana, the province, the territory, the state, used black soldiers more than did the English colonies which became the thirteen original United States. In 1729, there were about two thousand black slaves scattered throughout the then French colony but largely concentrated in the vicinity of New Orleans. In that year, the Natchez Indians attacked the French settlement at Natchez and killed over two hundred settlers. The Governor at New Orleans had only sixty able-bodied soldiers with which to defend the entire colony. In true frontier style, he called up all of the settlers along with the slaves owned by the French trading company active in that region. The Governor used special units of the slaves against the Indians. Black volunteers wiped out a nearby tribe of Chaouacha Indians and other black militiamen earned their freedom carrying messages to posts up the Mississippi. After the war, the French authorities on the scene recommended granting immediate freedom to all slaves who fought against the Indians and that "a company be formed of free Negroes." The French did activate such a militia company in the 1730s, for service in later Indian wars and even slaves were enrolled in it.

Militia companies of free blacks also participated in the American Revolution. By then New Orleans was under Spanish rule, but the Spanish in the Caribbean were willing to use black soldiers in the defense of their empire. At least one black unit stayed in the militia system after the revolution. That company fought escaped slaves in the Cimarron War of 1784. Later, in a still-traditional role of the militia, the black militia helped in civic action when in the spring of 1790, they assisted in repairing crevasses in the levees along the Mississippi River. Both of those activities were done alongside white militiamen. The Spanish governor, during that decade, increased the number of black noncommissioned officers in the two peacetime companies of black militia. Between September 1792 and May 1794, he issued twenty-nine promotions to the grades of corporal and sergeant. The bulk of the promotions were made as part of Spain's 1793 preparations for war with France. The units continued to be recognized by the Spanish government until 1803 when France resumed jurisdiction over the colony. The French administrators also knew the value of the units and continued them in a recognized status.

The very existence of those units created a problem for the new United States administration when it took over the territory of Louisiana from the French later in 1803. No parallel body of black militia existed under normal peacetime conditions in the then United States. On the other hand, as the new Governor, William C. C. Claiborne, pointed out to President Thomas Jefferson, the loyalty of the black Louisianians to the new territorial government was as much a concern as the loyalty of the white citizens. The militiamen themselves took the next step. They signed a petition attesting to their loyalty to the United States and volunteered their units for duty under the new regime. Many of the local citizens objected to the continuing existence of the unit, even under all white officers. The controversy ended in 1812 when, under the pressure of the outbreak of the War of 1812, the state legislature authorized the activation of a battalion known first as the Battalion of Chosen Men of Color, later as the Battalion of Free Men of Color. Significantly, the governor was also authorized to commission black officers as long as the battalion's commanding officer was white.

Probably the most famous campaign of the historic black militia of New Orleans was their participation in the Battle of New Orleans under the over-all command of Major General Andrew Jackson.

On 5 August 1814 General Jackson asked the governors of Louisiana, Tennessee and the Mississippi Territory to prepare their assigned quotas of militia for active duty. Governor Claiborne, in his response, offered to raise a corps of three or four hundred free blacks as part of the Louisiana militia activated for service against the British. After the usual correspondence, proclamations, and allaying of suspicions raised by worried white leaders, several black units participated in the defense of New Orleans. In addition to the Battalion of Free Men of Color, Major Louis Daquin raised a battalion of volunteer black refugees from Santo Domingo (now the Dominican Republic) and the black Captain Gabriel Gerome organized a home guard company of 79 overage free blacks.

Major Daquin's battalion participated in Jackson's surprise night attack of 23 December on the advancing British. Although causing severe casualties, that attack did not stop the enemy. By 23 December, Major Pierre Lacoste's Battalion of Free Men of Color was in the final defensive line along with Major Daquin's men, the white militia, the regulars, the Marines, and the pirates. Thus, the black battalions were in the line when the British began their final assault upon New Orleans on the fateful morning of 8 January 1815. Not directly in front of the British advance, the two battalions took most of their casualties after the battle when they attempted to retrieve the wounded of both sides and when they volunteered to clear the field of British sharpshooters.

The Battalions slowly faded out of existence after the War of 1812. Although their veterans were feted in New Orleans until the Civil War, by 1865 the military service of those black volunteers free and slave who had served in a tradition begun in 1729 in the organized militia of Louisiana had faded from the popular mind, and a new era was about to begin in American life.

—Martin K. Gordon

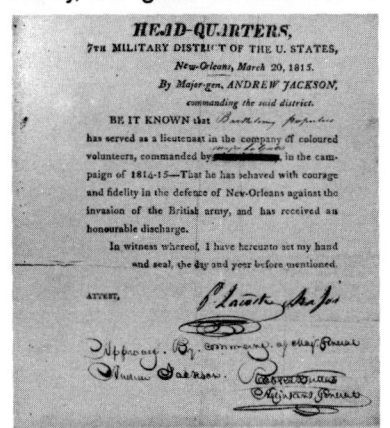

National Archives
An honorable discharge certificate for a black officer of the Battalion of Free Men of Color

THE BATTALION OF FREE MEN OF COLOR

BIBLIOGRAPHY

Kaplan, Sidney. *The Black Presence in the Era of the American Revolution*. New York: New York Graphic Society, Ltd., in Association with the Smithsonian Institution Press, 1973.

McConnell. Roland C. *Negro Troops of Antebellum Louisiana: A History of the Battalion of Free Men of Color*. Baton Rouge: Louisiana State University Press, 1968.

Nell, William C. *Services of Colored Americans in the Wars of 1776 and 1812*. Philadelphia: A.M.E. Publishing House, 1894.

The author acknowledges with gratitude the advice of Professor Roland C. McConnell in the preparation of this essay.

This essay originally appeared in the February 1977 *Push Pin Post*.

A PRELUDE TO BRAVERY

Blacks participated in the first defense forces of the new Ohio territory of the 1780s. Because of the frequent Indian raids upon the white settlements, the territorial assembly legally enrolled blacks in the militia. Whites' fear of the Shawnee, Ottawa, and Wyandott Indians overshadowed concern about armed blacks. Eleven years later, in 1799 however, the legislature inserted the word "white" into the legal qualifications for participation in the militia. A combination of the racial requirements of a new Federal militia act and growing race prejudice, especially in southern Ohio, would hold power and keep blacks from participating in the militia as they wanted to do for the next sixty-four years.

The leadership of the black community in Ohio had two political goals in the long decades before the Civil War: the right to vote and the right to participate in the militia. Both were signs of equality. At the state's 1850–1851 Constitutional Convention, these issues caused major clashes. One delegate, William Sawyer of Auglaize County, unwittingly linked two causes that were to develop a century or more later when he declared that if blacks were permitted in the militia, he would support a state constitutional amendment permitting women to bear arms. Another proposal would allow blacks to hold militia musters but only in cold weather. That proposal implied that blacks could only soldier in warm temperatures. That Convention wrote the ban against black participation in the militia into the state constitution.

The light-skinned mulatto leadership of the black community defined itself as an elite in several ways. They belonged to either the Free and Accepted Masons or the Elks, they supported President Lincoln, and they officered unrecognized militia companies. That "militia aristocracy" succeeded in getting 5,092 Ohio blacks officially mustered into federal service during the Civil War.

On April 12, 1861 the Ohio legislature first heard that the rebels had fired on Fort Sumter. Seven days later a Cleveland black militia company meeting in secret session volunteered its services to the government. Later the same month, the leading mulatto families of Albany, Ohio organized the "Attucks Guards" and volunteered for active duty. Governor William Dennison, opposed to trusting black militia forces, passed their tenders of service to the state's adjutant general, Carthinius Buckingham, who declined their offers on the grounds that the state constitution forbade state recognition of black militia units. Incidentally, the enthusiasms and frustrations of the first years of the Civil War helped to heal the breach between the mulatto and darker-skinned blacks in Ohio.

Black volunteers reacted to this official prejudice in several ways. Some light-skinned blacks simply passed for white and entered officially all-white regiments. Thus, the honor of being the first black Ohioan to enlist in the Civil War probably goes to John H. Cisco of Cleveland. He enrolled as a white soldier in the 124th Ohio Volunteer Infantry and in August 1861 was promoted to corporal in Company "F". Others in 1863 went to New England to enlist in the soon-to-be-famous Massachusetts black 54th and 55th Volunteer Infantry Regiments.

As has been true in other wars, manpower shortages eventually forced the enrollment of black militiamen. The attitude of September, 1862, when Governor David Tod had refused the offer of a black regiment to defend Cincinnati when the Confederates threatened the city, changed. At that time blacks were organized into a "Black Brigade" for fatigue duty in preparing fortifications for the city but the regiment was not called to arms. In early 1863, the federal government had established the Bureau of Colored Troops, black soldiers had begun to prove themselves under fire, and perhaps most importantly, Massachusetts had already enlisted 1700 Ohio black volunteers. Governor Tod decided that spring to raise a black regiment and he soon had his thousand men. On June 18, 1863, this new force was designated the 127th Ohio Volunteer Infantry Regiment, later the 5th Regiment, United States Colored Troops (USCT). In January 1864, Ohio raised a second black regiment, the 27th USCT. Both regiments participated in major campaigns such as the Wilderness Campaign of 1864 as well as the minor skirmishes which cause casualties but seldom make the history books. Both Buckeye regiments participated in the battles for Petersburg, the 5th in an assault on June 15, and the 27th in a follow-on wave to the initial assault after the Union mine exploded to open the Confederate lines on July 30. In 1865, both regiments participated in the capture of Fort Fisher, North Carolina. Meanwhile, four black NCOs of the 5th USCT had earned the Congressional Medal of Honor at New Market Heights, Virginia on September 29, 1864.

The pre-war struggles for recognition of the black Guardsmen of Ohio would have to be repeated in the years to come. These efforts are their prelude to the bravery they displayed in the wars of the United States.

—Martin K. Gordon

National Archives
The Union's IX Corps charging into the Crater opened by the explosion of the mine on 30 July 1864. Ohio's 27th United States Colored Troops participated in this attack.

A PRELUDE TO BRAVERY

BIBLIOGRAPHY

Black, Lowell D.   "The Negro Volunteer Units of the Ohio National Guard, 1870-1954: The Struggle for Military Recognition and Equality in the State of Ohio." Ph. D. dissertation, Ohio State University, 1976. Also available through Military Affairs/Aerospace Historian Press, Manhattan, Kansas.

Covers a longer time period than indicated in the title.

Cullen, Joseph P. "The Siege of Petersburg!" *Civil War Times Illustrated* 9 (August 1970): 3-50.

A special issue.

Pleasants, Henry, Jr.   *The Tragedy of the Crater*. n. p.: Eastern National Park & Monument Association, 1975, Reprint of 1938 edition.

This essay originally appeared in the February 1978 *Push Pin Post*.

Black History Month: A Time For Remembering

A nation's history, just like an individual's memory, is selective. There is just more information than we can absorb, so we pick and choose. Sometimes these choices are purposeful, sometimes they are a product of unconscious feelings. America is committed to erasing the taint of racial discrimination and segregation. This is a worthy commitment, but sometimes it leads us to erase from our consciousness part of our national experience. It is easy to forget institutions that were a product of racial separation. We in the National Guard are no different in this respect. How quickly we have forgotten the tradition of the black militia.

February is black history month. There is no better time to remind ourselves of the part played by Black Americans in the militia and National Guard. For as the National Guard was, and is, a part of the social fabric of white America, so black militia and National Guard units were part and parcel of the social fabric of black America. It is worthwhile to reconsider this piece of Guard history. The story is today only in bits and pieces. But we would like to share with you the history of one group of Black Guardsmen.

Two acts by Congress, one deleting racial restrictions from the militia law, and the other, extending full civil rights to the black community of the Nation's capital, paved the way for the organization of the black militia in Washington, D.C. just after the Civil War. The first of these units to organize, probably, was the Butler Zouaves, named after Civil War General, Benjamin F. Butler, and the Stanton Guards named after the Secretary of War. The Butler Zouaves went on to enter the District of Columbia National Guard as its Fifth Battalion in 1887. But, the Washington Cadet Corps organized as a single company in June, 1880 and expanded to four companies in 1885, was the first black unit to become a permanent component of the D.C. Guard. By the time of the National Drill Competition in Washington, D.C. in the summer of 1887 it had a total of 450 officers, men, and bandsmen. This unit's annual drill was one of the highlights of black Washington's social season. Its arch competitor for the affections of black Washingtonians was the Capitol City Guards, organized in 1883, and also destined to become a permanent part of the D.C. Guard. The Washington Cadet Corps was commanded by Major Christian A. Fleetwood, a black, Civil War Medal of Honor winner (his Medal of Honor is presently on exhibit in the Smithsonian Institution). Fleetwood, by the way, was so well-known in the national black community, that he was chosen to speak on "The Negro as a Soldier," at the Negro Congress at the 1895 Cotton States and International Exhibition in Atlanta, Georgia.

In 1889 the D.C. Guard was reorganized and the Washington Cadet Corps and the Capitol

Washingtoniana Division
Martin Luther King Memorial Library
Company A, Captain A. Brooks, Washington Cadet Corps, National Drill and Encampment, May 1887.

> We are all part of some minority, even though most of us never think of ourselves in this way. Southerners are in the minority, so are Catholics and Blacks and Jews and Hispanic-Americans and, in fact, white, Anglo-Saxon, Protestants. A pluralistic society is a polyglot of minorities. That's the way it is. But, all minorities are not treated in the same way. Therein lies the rub. Discrimination and racial prejudice against Black Americans are woven into the fabric of American life and it is hard to pull out the pernicious threads without unraveling the whole fabric. But as America is committed to eliminating racial discrimination, so is the National Guard. Substantial progress has been made. Between November 1974 and November 1975 Black participation in the National Guard has increased by one third. The totals are still not high, but the improvement is dramatic. We expect the National Guard to reflect the ethnic and racial composition of the community. That's the American way and that's the National Guard way.

Library of Congress
Christian A. Fleetwood, Civil War Medal of Honor winner, who as Captain and later Major commanded the Washington Cadet Corps from its organization in 1880 until its consolidation with the Capital City Guards in 1891.

City Guards lost two companies each. This was a serious blow to the morale of the two units, but the Adjutant General at the time, Brigadier General Albert Ordway justified the move on the grounds of declining enrollments and the failure of Congress to appropriate enough funds. Two years later the First Separate Battalion was formed. It was composed of the old Cadet Corps and the Capitol City Guards. But, it took an uproar from the black community to force the Guard to keep any of its black units.

When the Spanish-American War broke out most of the D.C. Guard was mobilized. However, the First Separate Battalion was rejected for active service. The reason was simple, it was black. But, two decades later this would not happen again. In 1916 the unit was mobilized and sent to Naco, Arizona, when war with Mexico seemed like a distinct possibility. They were among the first troops assigned to the Mexican border and immediately relieved regular Army troops. Their job was to guard the Naco water works which provided vitally needed water to five or six local communities.

A year later the battalion was mobilized once again to guard Washington, D.C. when it appeared that America was finally going to enter World War I. In 1918 the unit was sent to France as part of the 372nd Infantry Regiment, where it fought valiantly as part of the French Army. The D.C. Guard's First Separate Battalion was more than "an expression of the club or fraternity spirit" that motivated so many militiamen, "it was a first rate combat unit," wrote one historian.

The history of the black militia of the District of Columbia continued until well after World War II, but times were changing and racial segregation was swiftly coming to an end. Today, the tradition of these valiant Guardsmen lives on in many of the units of the D.C. Guard, but the days of separate and unequal are over. Many other states had black militia units. Some of those were Connecticut, Illinois, Maryland, New York, and almost all of the Southern States where black militia units were organized to protect reconstruction governments. Many of these southern units, it might be added, outlived reconstruction.

The history of racial segregation is not a pleasant one. But, out of necessity grew institutions that all Americans can take pride in. The black militia is one of those institutions that all National Guard members can be proud of. They served the country and the National Guard well.

Story from "The Black Militia in the District of Columbia," by Martin K. Gordon in the *Records of the Columbia Historical Society, James E. Walker* by Paul Edw. Sluby, Jr. and *The Negro as a Soldier*, by Christian A. Fleetwood.
NGB-IC-76-11 PP-ME 76

BLACK HISTORY MONTH: A TIME FOR REMEMBERING

BIBLIOGRAPHY

Fleetwood, Christian A. The Negro as a Soldier. Washington, DC: Howard University Print., 1895.

Gordon, Martin K. "The Black Militia in the District of Columbia, 1867-1898." Records of the Columbia Historical Society, 1971-1972 (Washington: Columbia Historical Society, 1973): 411-420.

Sluby, Paul Edward, Sr. A Biography of Major James Edward Walker, 1874-1918. Washington, DC: Printed at the Armstrong Adult Center, 1973.

This essay originally appeared as a special feature in the February 1976 Push Pin Post.

The Milicias Disciplinadas De Puerto Rico
THE TRAINED MILITIA OF PUERTO RICO

As does so much in the military, this story begins with a staff study. Alejandro O'Reilly, the famous Irish soldier in the pay of the King of Spain, filed a report on the condition of the troops and fortifications of Puerto Rico in the middle 1760s. That report marks the beginnings of the Puerto Rico National Guard. Acting on his own report, O'Reilly reorganized and trained the militia. He restructured the force into 19 companies of infantry and five of cavalry. He also gave it the name of the *Milicias disciplinadas.* Four years later, the militia was partially reorganized into four battalions and redesignated the *Cuerpo de milicias disciplinadas de infanteria de Puerto Rico*. In 1797 during a war with England, another reorganization saw a regimental structure for the Puerto Rican forces develop. The 295th and 296th regiments of today's Puerto Rico National Guard date from that era of warfare and experimentation.

That early *Regimiento* underwent several reorganizations during the 19th century, most of them tending to de-emphasize this Puerto Rican unit in favor of the Spanish-born militia. Finally, in 1870 this regiment was replaced by battalions of *Voluntarios urbanos* who were presumed to be more loyal to the colonial system during that century of revolutionary turmoil in the Spanish Empire.

Although the trained militia *(Milicias Disciplinadas)* and the City Corps *(Cuerpo de Urbanos)* were distinct organizations, they both drew on the same universal requirement for military service that applied at that time in the United States to white men. There was that notable difference, however. The black militia in the United States, centered in the Battalion of Free Men of Color in New Orleans (see February's PUSH PIN POST) was gradually being phased out of existence while black volunteers were permitted in the Puerto Rican militia. For example, in 1869 there were 18 white and mulatto *(blancos y pardos)* companies of infantry throughout the island and one black *(morenos)* company in Bayamon. There were also five companies of cavalry reported that year but no artillery. Interestingly, a later history mentions an excellent black artillery battery of eight cannon in Cangrejos (the *artilleros morenos de Cangrejos*). The *Milicias disciplinadas* was disbanded in 1870. The *Voluntarios* reported a strength of 5,446 in 1893, five years before the Spanish-American War, however. But due to the disbanding of the *Milicias,* no Puerto Rican, as distinct from Spanish, units opposed the 1898 invasion of the United States forces who conquered the island in that war.

The 65th Infantry, PRNG, dates its origins back to that period of Army control of the territory. Originally a Regular Army unit, the 65th was transferred to the Puerto Rico Army National Guard in 1959.

Congress, 3 June 1916, authorized the formal establishment of the Puerto Rico National Guard and thus began its modern era. A young officer, Luis Raul Esteves, destined to serve from 1919 to 1958 as the highest ranking officer of the Puerto Rico National Guard, led the agitation. To spur the organization of the force he wanted, Esteves published in 1918 the first edition of his *Manual del Soldado Puertorriqueño*. The *Manual* went through several editions and was in use at least to the outbreak of the Second World War. On 30 June 1940, the PRNG was able to report a strength of 104 officers and 1,886 men.

Within this evolution, the 295th Infantry, descendant of the *Milicias* was given its current designation 23 January 1923. Its 1st and 2d Battalions were reorganized and redesignated 1 June 1936 as the 296th Infantry but kept the same proud lineage of the 1760s *Milicias*.

The two regiments were federalized 15 October 1940 for service in World War II. The 295th saw service in the American Theater which included preparations in 1943 for an amphibious assault on Martinique which was later cancelled. The 296th saw service in both the American and Asiatic-Pacific Theaters. Both regiments along with the 65th Infantry remain in existence today.

As these forces continued to evolve, they were joined by the Puerto Rico Air National Guard. During the 1962 Cuban crisis, eight of its units under the 156th Fighter Group (Air Defense) stood ready, and its combat-ready pilots, aircraft, and radar sites were utilized. For their services, the Air National Guardsmen received the Caribbean Emergency Ribbon.

From the sails of the Spanish Empire to the jets of the modern age, from *Milicias* to Guardsmen, the citizens of Puerto Rico have fully participated in the heritage of the citizen-soldier.

—Martin K. Gordon

The first two newly assigned A-7D Corsairs are escorted by PRANG F-104 aircraft upon their arrival at San Juan, P.R. on 26 September 1975.

THE MILICIAS DISCIPLINADAS DE PUERTO RICO
THE TRAINED MILITIA OF PUERTO RICO
BIBLIOGRAPHY

Conn, Stetson, Engleman, Rose C., and Fairchild, Byron. Guarding the United States and its Outposts. The United States Army in World War II: The Western Hemisphere Series. Washington: Government Printing Office, 1964.

See pages 438-441 for the work of Puerto Rican forces.

Cordero Dávila, Juan César, Maj. Gen. "Puerto Rico National Guard." Army Information Digest (November 1964): 52-60.

Dorda y Lopez, Ramon Hermosa. Cartilla del voluntario de la isla de Puerto-Rico. Puerto Rico: Sucesión de J. J. Acosta, 1893.

Esteves, Luis Raul, Brig. Gen. Manual del Soldado Puertoriqueño. San Juan: Bureau of Supplies, Printing, and Transportation, 1939.

Padrón, Antonio E. El 65 en Revista: Datos Históricos, Relatos y Anecdotas, Tipos y Cuentos del Regimiento. New York: Las Americas Pub. Co., 1961.

Puerto Rico. Adjutant General. Annual Report of the Adjutant General of Puerto Rico for Fiscal Year ending June 30, 1940. San Juan: Bureau of Supplies, Printing, and Transportation, 1940.

Rivero Méndez, Angel, Capt. Crónica de la Guerra Hispano Americana en Puerto Rico. Madrid: Sucesores de Rivadeneyra (s.a.) artes gráficas, 1922.

See chapter XXX, "Resena Histórica del Servicio Militar en Puerto Rico."

Spain. War Office. Organización y Estado Militar de España y Ultramar. Madrid: Imprenta y Litografía del Depósito de la Guerra, 1869.

U. S. Army. Center of Military History. Organizational History Branch. "Unit Files: 65th Infantry, 295th Infantry, 296th Infantry."

This essay was originally published in the September 1977 Push Pin Post.

The New Mexico militia in the Civil War

New Mexico was the Confederate gateway to either the bullion mines of Colorado or the Pacific Ocean ports of California. But they could cross that territory only after defeating the combination of regular soldiers, and New Mexico, Colorado, and later California state forces that stood in their path. The great majority of the New Mexico forces were of Hispanic origin and had only been United States citizens from the time of the transfer of the territory to the U.S. at the end of the War with Mexico in 1848.

When military action began in New Mexico during the summer of 1861, both commanders, Colonel Edward R. S. Canby, USA, and Brigadier General Henry H. Sibley, CSA, were organizing their forces. Canby consolidated his remaining regulars at two major posts, asked the governors of New Mexico and Colorado for volunteer units for varying periods of service, and asked the governor of New Mexico to call up the approximately 1000 largely Hispanic militiamen then enrolled. The War Department authorized the raising of six volunteer regiments in New Mexico. After a fast turnover, Colonel Christopher "Kit" Carson, the Indian fighter, took command of the First New Mexico Volunteers, while Colonel Miguel Pino took the Second Volunteers, the first of these units to be organized.

Canby displayed his lack of faith in the New Mexico forces when he issued them older weapons and inferior quality uniforms. He did not feel that he could rely on the Hispanic New Mexicans unless they were stiffened by regulars or volunteers from some other region. He also doubted the political loyalty of these new citizens.

The first major battle of the campaign was fought at the Valverde fort of the Rio Grande, six miles above Fort Craig. The Valverde Fort, where one of the major battles was fought, was the key defensive position between the invading Texans and the towns of Albuquerque and Santa Fe. On February 19, 1862, just before the battle, Colonel Canby sent Carson's and Pino's regiments to guard a high spot between the two armies. The next day Canby attacked with these regiments supported by cavalry and artillery.

The 21st saw the Battle of Valverde proper. The Union advanced across the river with regular and volunteer cavalry support by artillery and infantry. The assault force included the cavalry of the Third New Mexico Volunteers under Lieutenant Colonel José M. Valdez along with two New Mexico infantry companies. The Confederate cavalry soon saw the force and attacked. The heavy artillery and small-arms fire that marked the day now began. After an afternoon pause, the Confederates attacked and were repulsed on the Union right. The pursuit began on that side and a large gap opened in the Union center. Then the main Confederate attack hit the Union artillery on the left. Canby ordered both regular and state forces to advance. Pino's regiment, advancing to the support of the artillery, was crossing the river when the brunt of the Confederate attack came down on that spot. They retreated, but by then both regulars and volunteers were in flight, panicking the men behind them. Canby was forced to abandon the battlefield and retreat into Fort Craig.

Canby ignored the flight of some of his regulars and complained that he would have won if only the New Mexico forces had advanced upon his orders. He certainly had not worried about their morale before the battle when he gave them old weapons and inferior quality uniforms and had not accepted them as line soldiers. Canby, in spite of the fact that some Hispanic units had fought well, criticized them all as an argument to obtain more regulars from the east.

Meanwhile, the campaign went on. Individual soldiers stood out on both sides; many of these were Hispanic members of the New Mexico militia. One of the most notable was Lieutenant Colonel Manuel Chávez who helped achieve a decisive Union victory during the Battle of Gloriéta Pass, March 28, 1862. Chávez, a New Mexico volunteer who had fought at Valverde, guided a force of regular and Colorado soldiers through the mountains around the Confederate lines to the Confederate supply camp. As a result, an entire Confederate supply train was captured and the Confederates retreated, crippled by the loss of their supplies.

The official list of New Mexico volunteers during the Civil War shows 4,327 Spanish names. The Civil War that represented brother against brother was also a war of hermano en frente de hermano. Other Americans of Spanish ancestry served in the Colorado Volunteers. The Hispanic tradition of military service to the United States that began before the Civil War and continues to this day, has contributed significantly to building the nation we know today.

— Martin K. Gordon

Fort Craig as it appeared during the 1870's. It was garrisoned by Hispanic-American citizen-soldiers during part of the Civil War. (Photo courtesy of the National Archives)

THE NEW MEXICO MILITIA IN THE CIVIL WAR

BIBLIOGRAPHY

Anderson, Latham. "Canby's Services in the New Mexican Campaign." *Battles and Leaders of the Civil War*. II: 697-699.

   This volume also contains several other accounts of the episodes discussed in this essay.

Hall, Martin H. *Sibley's New Mexico Campaign*. Austin: Univ. of Texas Press, 1960.

Harris, Gertrude. *A Tale of Men Who Knew Not Fear*. San Antonio: Alamo Printing Co., 1935.

Kerby, Robert L. *The Confederate Invasion of New Mexico and Arizona, 1861-1862*. Los Angeles, CA: Westernlore Press, 1958.

Myers, Lee. "Military Activities in the Mesilla Valley." *Periodical* 9 (Winter 1977-78): 43-52.

--------. "New Mexico Volunteers." *Periodical* 4(Fall-Winter 1972):23-27.

Thompson, Jerry D. *Colonel John Robert Baylor: Texas Indian Fighter and Confederate Soldier*. Hill Junior College Monograph No. 5. Hillsboro, TX: Hill Junior College, 1971.

Whitford, William C. *Colorado Volunteers in the Civil War: The New Mexico Campaign in 1862*. Denver: The State Historical and Natural History Society, 1906; reprint ed., Glorieta, NM: The Rio Grande Press, Inc., 1971.

Wright, Arthur A. *The Civil War in the Southwest*. Denver: Big Mountain Press, 1964.

OTHER RECENT STUDIES

Miller, Darlis A. "Hispanos and the Civil War in New Mexico: A Reconsideration." *New Mexico Historical Review* 54 (April 1979): 105-123.

Myers, Lee. *New Mexico Military Installations*. Globe, AZ: Southwest Parks and Monuments Assoc., n.d.

   The Tucson Corral of the Westerners is publishing Mr. Myers' study of the New Mexico Volunteers in its journal *Smoke Signal*.

Perrine, David P. "The Battle of Valverde, New Mexico Territory, February 21, 1862." In LeRoy H. Fischer, ed.; *Civil War Battles in the West*. Manhattan, KS: Sunflower Univ. Press, 1981. Pp. 26-38.

Mr. Lee Myers commented that a study of the *Official Records of the War of the Rebellion*, particularly Canby's report in vol. IX, might provide a different interpretation of Sibley's Campaign. Myers said that only a small number of regulars fled during the battle of Valverde. Furthermore, Canby did not deliberately provide the militia with inferior equipment, but supplied what he had. A lack of war materials crippled Canby. Also, additional study must be made of the muster rolls before the service of large numbers of Americans of Spanish ancestry in the Colorado Volunteers can be documented. The author acknowedges the advice of Mr. Myers and his permission to summarize it here.

ERRATUM

The name of the ford, not fort, in the fourth paragraph should read Valverde ford.

This essay originally appeared in the September 1979 *Push Pin Post*.

Jews, Discrimination and the Militia

In the American colonial period with its established churches, there was often a belief that those who didn't conform to the state church, or like the Jews, didn't believe in Christianity at all, should not be permitted to hold military office under that government. This belief was to remain embedded in the Maryland constitution until the 1800s. An extreme example of this old-world prejudice in the colonial American militia system took place in New Amsterdam, later New York, in 1655. The governor, Peter Stuyvesant, and the New Amsterdam Council on August 28, adopted a resolution excluding the Jews from military service in the town's Burgher Guard. Two reasons were given: "the disinclination and unwillingness of the trainbande to be fellow soldiers with the aforesaid nation and to be on guard with them in the same guardhouse;" and, because Jews were not admitted to this duty in Amsterdam nor in any city of the Netherlands. Instead of military service, each adult male Jew was required to pay a heavy tax each month.

That November two Jews, Jacob Barinson and Asser Levy, petitioned the Council to either let them join the town guard or exempt them from the tax as they could not afford to pay it. The authorities rejected the petition. However, it is not clear whether that discriminatory resolution was ever enforced fully. By the spring of 1657, Asser Levy and other Jews were serving in the Burgher Guard like any other citizens.

By 1776 this legal prejudice had died out to a considerable extent and Jews participated on both sides of the American Revolution. They served in both the Continental Army and the state militias. During the war scare of 1808, the Jews of Charleston, South Carolina volunteered as a separate company and wore a distinctive uniform similar to that of the city cavalry. Later, Jewish Colonel Nathan Myers commanded a brigade stationed near New York City at the outbreak of the War of 1812.

Discrimination in the militia after the American Revolution against the Jew seemed to be most active in Maryland. The Maryland Constitution of 1777 required an oath that no Jew could conscientiously take: that the oath of office be taken upon the truth faith of a Christian. That requirement of course included those who wanted to hold a militia officer's commission from that state.

Apparently that law was not always enforced, however. During the militia revival of 1798, when war with France seemed close, the Baltimore San Culottes, an infantry company named after one of the elements active in the French Revolution, met and changed its name to the Baltimore Independent Blues. Its Jewish Lieutenant, Reuben Etting, was elected captain during that period. Apparently Etting served in both grades without concern over his religious background.

Several Baltimore Jews served in the ranks of local units in the defense of Baltimore during the War of 1812. In 1817-1818, the state began to debate in earnest the changing of the qualifying oath of office so as to enable Jews to hold state offices and commissions. Both Jewish petitioners to the legislature and its pre-reform members reminded the other legislators of the Jews' service in past wars and the unfairness of denying a well-earned commission to a soldier just because of his religion.

As this debate continued, the Marion Rifles was organized in Baltimore in the spring of 1823 and Benjamin I. Cohen, a private at Fort McHenry during the British bombardment there in 1814, was elected its captain. The Governor, Samuel Stevens, Jr., duly commissioned Cohen who could not accept the commission because of the required oath. Cohen then resigned his commission but the company would not accept the resignation until the legislature made up its mind about removing the discriminatory oath. The company first lieutenant commanded the unit until the legislature acted and changed the law.

Finally, January 5, 1826, by a 45-32 vote, the bill to abolish this religious test for office passed the legislature and became law. Benjamin Cohen, through Governor Stevens, presented a flag to his rifle company. In 1836 Governor Thomas W. Veazey commissioned Mendes I. Cohen as a colonel in the Maryland militia to serve as a governor's aide in recognition of his services during the War of 1812. In 1848 a company of volunteers was raised from the Jewish community in Baltimore to fight in the Mexican War and in an ironic twist elected a non-Jew as its captain.

Thus by the late 1840s, another form of ethnic discrimination had faded out of the militia as it continued to evolve into the present-day integrated National Guard.

Martin K. Gordon.

NGB-IC-76-80

JEWS, DISCRIMINATION AND THE MILITIA

BIBLIOGRAPHY

Altfeld, E. Milton. *The Jew's Struggle for Religious and Civil Liberty in Maryland*. Baltimore: M. Curlander, 1924.

Fein, Issac M. *The Making of an American Jewish Community: The History of Baltimore Jewry from 1773 to 1920*. Philadelphia: Jewish Publication Society of America, 1971.

Glushakow, Abraham D. *A Pictorial History of Maryland Jewry*. Baltimore: Jewish Voice Pub. Co., 1955.

Sandler, Philip. "Earliest Jewish Settlers in New York." *New York History*. 36 (January 1955): 39-50.

Scharf, J. Thomas, Col. *The Chronicles of Baltimore: Being a Complete History of 'Baltimore Town' and Baltimore City from the Earliest Period to the Present Time*. Baltimore: Turnbull Brothers, 1874.

Wolf, Simon. *The American Jew as Patriot, Soldier and Citizen*. Philadelphia: The Levytype Company and New York: Brentano's, 1895.

The author wishes to acknowledge with gratitude the assistance of Dr. Moses Aberbach, Curator of the Jewish Historical Society of Maryland, Inc.

This essay originally appeared in the December 1976 *Push Pin Post*.

The Ethnic Militia of Early Milwaukee

Militia units based on a common ethnic or racial background were common during the nineteenth century heyday of distinctively uniformed and carefully trained volunteer units. The Emmett Zouaves were likely to be Irish, the Kosciuszko Guards Polish, and the Lincoln Light Infantry might be a Black unit.

Milwaukee, the premier city of the new state of Wisconsin, certainly reflected this heritage in the years before the Civil War. In January, 1847, shortly after Milwaukee became a city, George E. Meffert and George Brosius organized the first militia unit, the Milwaukee Rifle Company. Formation of this predominantly German unit was followed shortly by the organization of the City Guard, composed mainly of Third Ward Irish. By the outbreak of the Civil War, Milwaukee had two Irish companies, five German units and one "American" outfit, the Milwaukee Light Guard.

Some of these units faded over the years as was natural for the volunteer units of the era. In April 1851, a "Reverend" E. Leahy came to Milwaukee claiming to be a defrocked monk. Several hundred Irish Catholics turned out to break up his talk while a large number of Protestants fought them before, during, and after the speech. The mayor, the constables, and the fire department had to join with individual volunteers to protect the speaker. According to one historian of the event, the only active militia units in the city that year were Irish and could not be depended upon to defend Leahy. The Germans had not kept up their units and hence could not be called out.

Ethnic problems continued to plague the city in the years that followed.

Tension had been building over elections in which Germans, Irish, and native-born Americans all contested local offices over such concerns as temperance and patronage. On Tuesday, March 7, 1854 those tensions peaked.

An Irish pollwatcher that election day challenged the right of a German to vote in the predominantly German First Ward. As the accounts go, the German then proceeded to grab the Irishman and hit him. Other Irishmen present retaliated in kind. Then the Germans in the area plunged into the growing melee. There had previously been violence on election days, but nothing like this. Hundreds pitched in on both sides. The Irish held the polling place while the Germans held the surrounding buildings. Stones and bricks flew back and forth as Irish and Germans alike supported their countrymen. The sheriff was badly hurt and the town's small police force was unable to do anything. One constable called to the scene even joined the mob (his nationality is unrecorded).

Where was the militia during all this? The authorities were afraid to call out the citizen-soldiers. Tensions were so high it was feared the units of the two sides would start firing upon each other if they were given the chance. It was thought safer not to have the armed militiamen on the streets during the disturbance. Several people were seriously injured and rumors of death spread on both sides. Eventually the riot ended.

Uncontrolled violence gave impetus to the nativist movement which grew in Milwaukee as elsewhere in the country. Within a year of the riot, one of the more permanent of the city's militia companies, which later became a battalion and then a regiment, was formed. The Milwaukee Light Guard adopted its constitution in October 1855. That document required United States citizenship for membership and marked the permanent beginnings of a non-ethnic militia in Milwaukee.

—Martin K. Gordon

Uniforms of the Milwaukee Light Guard, 1859 (photograph courtesy of the Milwaukee County Historical Society)

THE ETHNIC MILITIA OF EARLY MILWAUKEE

BIBLIOGRAPHY

Buck, James S. *Pioneer History of Milwaukee* and *Milwaukee Under The Charter*. 4 vols., rev. ed. Milwaukee: Swain & Tate, Printers, 1888-1890.

Damon, Herbert C. *History of the Milwaukee Light Guard*. Milwaukee: Printed by the Sentinel Company, 1875.

Flower, Frank A. *History of Milwaukee, Wisconsin*. Chicago: Western Historical Co., 1881.

Gordon, Martin K. "The Milwaukee Infantry Militia, 1865-1892." *Historical Messenger of the Milwaukee County Historical Society* 24 (March 1968): 2-15.

Gregory, John G. *History of Milwaukee, Wisconsin*. 4 vols. Chicago: J. J. Clark Pub. Co., 1931.

Still, Bayard. *Milwaukee: The History of a City*. Madison: The State Historical Society of Wisconsin, 1948.

This essay originally appeared in the September 1976 *Push Pin Post*.

ON BEING ALERT

This engraving of the capture of Fort Ticonderoga shows the summons to surrender given by Ethan Allen to Captain William De La Place of the 26th Cameronians. Obviously the post commander was taken by surprise.

The continual need for alert guards in the American military establishment is a point that cannot be made too often. Lazy or inadequate sentries have often made a difference during an unexpected raid. For example, during King William's War, 1689-1697, Connecticut sent 87 militia to reinforce New York strongpoints. Twenty-five of them were sent to Schenectady, then a frontier post containing about 150 Dutch traders and farmers and their black slaves in a stockaded village. Yet, with a war on, when a party of Canadians and Indians attacked the village on February 8, 1690, they found the gates guarded by only two snowmen. The raiders were able to kill 60 inhabitants and capture 27 more at a cost of only two killed.

On May 10, 1775, during the early stages of the American Revolution, a militia force composed of the Green Mountain Boys under Ethan Allen and other citizen-soldiers led by Colonel Benedict Arnold captured by surprise the thinly garrisoned Fort Ticonderoga. The militia entered along a cart path on the lake side of the fort through the wicket gate and were on the parade ground before a sentry challenged them. The fort was defended by 42 officers and men, only about half of whom were fit for duty, and also held 24 women and children. The post commander didn't even have time to fully dress before Ethan Allen was at his quarters demanding that he surrender the fort. This victory provided badly needed cannon for the revolutionary forces then besieging the British at Boston.

Sometimes, though, the bias of Regular vs. Guardsman creates different versions of the same event. The spring of 1916 saw the National Guard active on both the political and military fronts. Congress was debating what was to become the National Defense Act of 1916 and President Woodrow Wilson was mobilizing the National Guard for duty on the Mexican border.

Meanwhile, Mexican forces under Pancho Villa raided the town of Columbus, New Mexico, which was garrisoned by Regular cavalry, on March 9, 1916. The assault started around 0330 or 0400 when only the regular sentinels, the cooks, and the kitchen and stable police were awake. While these soldiers fought off the raiders, the rest of the garrison woke up and drove off the invaders, chasing them across the border. An investigation after that surprise raid cleared the regimental commander of charges of neglect of duty. But, that winter a letter appeared in the influential *Army and Navy Register* which was later reprinted in the *Congressional Record*. Signed "MILITIAMAN," It reflected both the importance of guard duty and the state of Regular - Guard relations at that time.

Militiaman wrote;

"We of the Organized Militia, who have been instructed in our military duties by the officers of the Regular Army ... have been impressed with the supreme importance of 'the service of security'; that is, of protecting a command ... against the invasion of marauders of any kind, and especially against a surprise attack by an armed and hostile force. We were astounded and shocked, therefore, to gather from newspaper accounts some time ago that this important service was so performed or neglected by a force of Regular troops stationed at Columbus, N. Mex., presumably for the protection of that town and its neighborhood against a possible and even probable raid ... that Villa and his small band could surprise both camp and town by a night attack and, after much burning, looting, and killing, could escape with but little punishment, taking with them as trophies a goodly number of horses that belonged to the troops that were supposed to be protecting the town."

The author went on to ask where were the patrols and sentinels that should have prevented such a surprise. He was astonished that the regiment and its commander had been exonerated of any blame for the surprise. He wrote:

"If National Guard troops had been so unfortunate or negligent in the discharge of their duties anywhere as were the Regular Army troops at Columbus is it likely that any special inspector could be found with hardihood enough to commend those troops for what they did or failed to do? On the contrary, is it not certain that those troops would have been condemned mercilessly as undisciplined and worthless militiaman?"

The anonymous author charged that the Washington end of the investigation had also been whitewashed. He claimed that the State and War Departments had had knowledge of this raid but had failed to notify the proper offices.

This militiaman failed to credit the regiment at Columbus for the heavy casualties they inflicted on the raiders while taking comparatively few themselves. He did, however, highlight the continual importance of alert patrols and sentinels while at the same time serve as a reminder of the hostility and mistrust that existed in times past between the Regulars and the Guard.

—Martin K. Gordon

ON BEING ALERT

BIBLIOGRAPHY

COLONIAL EPISODE

Peckham, Howard H. The Colonial Wars, 1689-1762. The Chicago History of American Civilization Series. Chicago: Univ. of Chicago Press, 1964.

THE AMERICAN REVOLUTION

Alden, John R. The American Revolution, 1775-1783. The New American Nation Series. New York: Harper & Row, Pubs., Harper Torchbooks, 1962.

Coakley, Robert W., and Conn, Stetson. The War of the American Revolution: Narrative, Chronology, and Bibliography. A Bicentennial Publication of the United States Army Center of Military History. Washington: Government Printing Office, 1975.

Higginbotham, Don. The War of American Independence: Military Attitudes, Policies, and Practice, 1763-1789. The Macmillan Wars of the United States Series. New York: The Macmillan Co., 1971.

Wallace, Willard M. Appeal To Arms: A Military History of the American Revolution. Chicago: Quadrangle Books, 1964.

TWENTIETH CENTURY

Clendenen, Clarence C. Blood on the Border: The United States Army and the Mexican Irregulars. The Macmillan Wars of the United States Series. New York: The Macmillan Co., 1969.

U. S. Congress. House. Debate on the Military Establishment. H. R. 12666. 64th Cong., 1st sess., 20 May 1916. Congressional Record, vol. 53.

_____. House. Debate on Army Appropriations. H. R. 20783. 64th Cong., 2d sess., 20 February 1917. Congressional Record, vol. 54.

This essay originally appeared in the December 1979 Push Pin Post.

The Oldest Of Them All:
The Massachusetts 101st. Eng. Bn And 182nd Infantry

Call-ups, formal musters, peacetime rescues and maintenance of order operations are the common lot of Guardsmen. But very few units can lay claim to have been performing these chores for over 340 years. The 101st Engineer Battalion was already 141 years old when, as Colonel John Glover's Marblehead Regiment, it rowed General George Washington and his staff across the Delaware on 25 December 1776. The 182d Infantry was 139 years old when it was called-up by Paul Revere and William Dawes during their famous ride on the night of 18 April 1775. The regiment was then known as the 1st Middlesex Regiment which, along with Gardner's Regiment, also from the Middlesex area, constituted the two Revolutionary War ancestors of the 182d.

These regiments, organized by an act of the General Court of Massachusetts Bay Colony dated 7 October 1636, hold older lineages than any units of the regular British Army. The General Court acted to reorganize the existing Train Bands under the twin pressures of population movement and the Pequot-Mohican War of 1636. The 101st Engineer Battalion was organized as the East Regiment and included militia from the towns of Saugus (Lynn), Salem, Ipswich, and Newbury. The 182d Infantry was organized as the North Regiment and included militia from the towns of Charlestown, New Town, Watertown, Concord, and Dedham.

Both units were active throughout the colonial period as the need arose. For example, the 101st fought in King George's War in 1745–48 against French Canada and again in 1755–63 during the French and Indian War. The 182d fought in King Philip's War in 1676 against the Wampanoag Indians and in King William's War of 1689–97 against the French and the Indians.

The Revolutionary War service of the two units is an index of the nearness of the War to New England. The 101st participated in the campaigns at Boston, Long Island, Trenton, Princeton, Monmouth, New York 1776, and the Rhode Island campaigns of 1777, 1778, and 1779. The 182d participated in the actions at Lexington, Boston, Quebec, Saratoga, and New York 1778 and 1779. It also participated in the War of 1812. Reflecting the opposition of their home state to the War with Mexico of 1847–48, neither unit participated in that conflict.

Indicative of Massachusetts' continued above average interest in her militia, both regiments participated in the rush to rescue the nation's capital at Washington at the outbreak of the Civil War. The Sixth Massachusetts Regiment of Infantry had been the first militia unit to arrive in Washington following the outbreak of the war, arriving 19 April 1861. The 101st Engineer Batallion, then designated the Eighth Regiment of Infantry, was mustered into active service 15 April 1861 and left for Washington three days later. The 182d Infantry, then the Fifth Regiment of Infantry was musturred into Federal service on 1 May 1861. The Eighth Massachusetts arrived in Washington on 26 April, one of the first four militia units to join the defenses of Washington during those nervous weeks. The Fifth was only a few days behind it. The 182d-Fifth Regiment fought well at the first Battle of Bull Run while the 101st-Eighth Regiment missed the battle, as did about a fourth of both armies that July day. The 182d-Fifth also saw action in the North Carolina Campaign of 1862 when it participated in the Union raid on Confederate rail and telegraph lines around Goldsboro. Both Regiments participated in the North Carolina Campaign of 1863.

Although both units were mustered into Federal service for the Spanish-American War of 1898, neither had time to participate in the campaigns of that short war. The Reading Militia, now the Headquarters Company of the 101st, did participate in action in Puerto Rico, however. Both regiments spent the summer of 1916 in Federal service for duty on the Mexican border.

The 101st contributed large numbers of personnel to 26th ("Yankee") Division units that fought in World War I, but as the 5th Pioneer Infantry Regiment it did not participate in any of the campaigns of that war. Its sister unit the 182d, then the 3d Pioneer Infantry, participated in the Meuse Argonne offensive.

Between the wars, floods in 1936 and a hurricane in 1938, kept these National Guardsmen busy.

The 101st was inducted into Federal

The Eighth Massachusetts Regiment, now the 101st Engineer Battalion, in the rotunda of the Capitol at Washington, May 1861. (Library of Congress)

service for duty in World War II on 16 January 1941 and redesignated from regimental size to the 101st Engineer Combat Battalion by 8 October 1942. That Battalion participated in the campaigns for Northern France, the Rhineland, the Ardennes-Alsace, and Central Europe. The 182d Infantry, known as such from 21 March 1923, joined the American Division to fight its way across the Asia-Pacific Theater. There, it reinforced the Marines during the bloody battle for Guadalcanal, fought in the Northern Solomons, landed during the fighting to Leyte in the Philippines, and landed later to fight to liberate the Southern Philippines.

Today, both units stand ready, as they have in the past, to carry out the words of the motto of the 182d, "Avitos Juvamus Honores," or "We Uphold Our Ancient Honors."

—Martin K. Gordon

THE OLDEST OF THEM ALL

THE MASSACHUSETTS 101st ENG BN and 182nd INFANTRY

BIBLIOGRAPHY

Catton, Bruce. The Centennial History of the Civil War. Vol. I: The Coming Fury. Garden City: Doubleday & Co., Inc., 1961.

Cooling, B. Franklin. Symbol, Sword, and Shield: Defending Washington During the Civil War. Hamden, CT: Archon Books, 1975.

Leech, Margaret. Reville in Wsshington, 1860-1865. New York: Time, Inc., 1962 Reprint of 1941 ed.

McBarron, H. Charles, Jr., and Peterson, Harold. "The North Regiment, Massachusetts Bay Colony, 1636." Military Collector & Historian. 4 (December 1952): 93-95.

Monahan, Tom. "Fountainhead of the Guard." Army Information Digest (March 1961): 46-53.

Peckham, Howard H. The Colonial Wars, 1689-1762. The Chicago History of American Civilization Series. Chicago: Univ. of Chicago Press, 1964.

U. S. Army. Center of Military History. Organizational History Branch, "Unit Files: 101st Engineer Battalion, 182d Infantry."

This essay originally appeared in the October 1977 Push Pin Post.

The Chatham Artillery: A Holiday Toast

Georgia's Chatham Artillery, also known as Headquarters and Headquarters Battery, 118th Field Artillery Group, Savannah, is well worthy of attention during this holiday season. Its parent regiment traces its roots back to an April 18, 1751 organization in the District of Savannah of four independent volunteer companies, three of infantry and one of cavalry. The Chatham Artillery itself dates from approximately 1785 and had in it many veterans of those earlier military organizations.

Thus, the Chatham Artillery is well-qualified to have originated its famous Chatham Artillery Punch out of both British and American traditions. Some have argued that the British Army's use of punches at festive occasions was also the beginning of the American forces' (both regular and volunteer) custom of distinctive unit drinks. Others have looked closely at the liquor allowance of the early American Army and decided that the ever ingenious soldier was simply trying to stretch his allowance, make it taste better, or make it more potent when these recipes and traditions were begun. Either or both sources could have been the origin of the Chatham's famous punch as the artillery was in contact with British military forces and was active in the formative years of American military traditions.

The Chatham militiamen passed through a number of reorganizations, common to that era, between the 1780s and the early 1800s. The beginnings of several present day Savannah units date from that period.

The Chatham Artillery was alerted in 1812 and mustered into federal service in 1815 for War of 1812 coastal defense duty. In state service, it participated in various Indian campaigns, and a sister company, the Irish Jasper Greens, was in federal service for the War with Mexico.

Savannah's volunteer companies organized their own Independent Volunteer Battalion in January 1852. This was a reorganization of the volunteer's Chatham Legion of 1820. The term "legion" meant to those soldiers what "combined arms" means today. Thus the Chatham Artillery was organic to that battalion with its six companies of colorfully named infantry: Savannah Volunteer Guards, Republican Blues, Phoenix Riflemen, Irish Jasper Greens, German Volunteers, and the DeKalb Riflemen. Four years later, in 1856, with the addition of the Oglethorpe Light Infantry, the battalion became a regiment.

The regiment was ordered into active state service at the start of the Civil War to take possession of Fort Pulaski in the Savannah harbor. During the war, the components of the regiments became

Captain John Wheaton, a mayor of Savannah, in his Chatham Artillery uniform. (Chatham Artillery)

the cadres for several new regiments, while the artillery was detached as an independent light battery. After participating in the defense of Savannah and of Charleston as well as campaigning in Florida, it surrendered April 26, 1865 near Greensboro, North Carolina. The unit continued to exist as a social corporation during the years when it was forbidden to drill while under arms.

In 1872, when it was again legally permissible for Georgia to maintain a militia, the former volunteer regiment reorganized as the 1st Regiment Georgia Volunteers, while the Chatham Artillery became a separate independent unit. It was mustered into federal service for the Spanish-American War. The Chatham Artillery also participated in World War I, but arrived in France too late to participate in the actual fighting.

In World War II, the Chathams, as part of the 30th Infantry Division's artillery, landed on the Normandy beaches on D-Day plus four and then fought their way across Europe to the Elbe River. The division and its artillery, in one particularly notable incident shortly after the landing, found itself in the center of a German counter-attack aimed through the village of Mortain to the Channel coast to divide the American forces into fragments. In six days of continuous action, the Chathams gave the Germans the feeling that the Americans had landed automatic artillery against them. The counter-attack was unsuccessful and the allies continued to push the Germans out of France.

Several post-war reorganizations, always common to the militia in peacetime, have produced the current designations of the Chatham Artillery as Headquarters and Headquarters Battery, 118th Field Artillery Group and as elements of the 214th Field Artillery. Whatever their current designations, the Chatham Artillery can be proud to include among its various military and civic contributions to the history of the National Guard its famous Chatham Artillery Punch.

POSTSCRIPT

The recipe is not given here for three reasons. First, the author does not want to encourage excessive drinking as the official recipe in his possession calls for making the punch in 12-gallon quantities. Second, there are variations on the basic recipe which may lead to disagreements about that formula. Third, the author does not want to slight any of the other historic recipes of the National Guard such as the Gin Horror, traditional among the enlisted men of the First Troop, Philadelphia City Cavalry, or the National Guard 7th Regiment Punch (NY), to give but two examples.

—Martin K. Gordon

THE CHATHAM ARTILLERY: A HOLIDAY TOAST

BIBLIOGRAPHY

Elting, John R., Col. "Artillery Punch: A Study in American Degeneracy." Military Collector & Historian 27 (Spring 1975): 35-36.

Peterson, Harold L. [Beveridge, N. E.]. Cups of Valor. Harrisburg: Stackpole Books, 1968.

An indispensable guide to the drinking habits of American soldiers.

[Quinney, H. M., Jr.] Chatham Artillery. Pub. by the Chatham Artillery, 1970.

Ruhlen, George, Maj. Gen. "Firepower and Punch." Field Artillery Journal (March-April 1977): 54-56.

U. S. Army. Center of Military History. Organizational History Branch. "Unit Files: components of 118th Field Artillery, 214th Field Artillery."

The author acknowledges with gratitude the assistance of Mr. George F. Hoffman, historian of the Chatham Artillery.

ERRATUM

The sketch of the punchbowl, cup, and dress covers in this essay is from Cups of Valor, reproduced here with permission of Stackpole Books.

This essay originally appeared in the December 1978 Push Pin Post.

Only You Can Save Your History:
The Saga of the Norwich Light Infantry

Just as in war the National Guard is in combat, so in peace it is continually reorganizing. The peacetime stress of trying to prepare for the next war while coping with shortages and economy drives leads to frequent reorganizations at various levels. One such reorganization almost cost the Connecticut ARNG part of its heritage. Fortunately, the implication of this proposed reorganization was understood and steps taken to save a detachment descended from the Revolutionary War actions of 1775. Indeed, through this action the non-honors displaying detachment now carries official honors as well as a lineage as a result of its timely redesignation.

The Norwich Light Infantry was organized in May 1775 under Captain Christopher Leffingwell, a member of the town's Committee of Correspondence. In 1776, the company marched to New York City as part of Connecticut's early contribution to George Washington's forces gathering for the defense of that city against the British. March 1777, the company turned out for the defense of New London, Connecticut against a British naval raid. They were then noted for "a martial appearance" and being "neatly dressed in uniforms." That summer they joined the Army massing at Fort Barton, Rhode Island for an intended expedition against the British at Aquidneck. Due to an unlucky combination of bad weather, not enough time being allowed for the arrival of supplies, and the inexperience of the commanding officer, that invasion was repulsed.

But the bloodiest action came September 6, 1781 when Benedict Arnold led a raiding force of 1,700 British, Loyalist, and German troops against New London, destroying 143 buildings and 12 ships. They overran Forts Trumbull and Griswold, killing 85 Americans, wounding 60, and capturing 70. Many of the casualties occurred in a massacre after the forts' surrender.

In a general reorganization of the Connecticut Militia in June 1847, this company became an artillery company in the state's volunteer militia. At the outbreak of the Civil War, it was mustered into federal service May 14, 1861 as Company D, 3d Connecticut Volunteer Infantry Regiment and rushed to the defense of Washington.

At the battle of First Bull Run, July 21, 1861, these new soldiers distinguished themselves in an otherwise dreary day. They spent the morning of the battle in Keyes's Brigade in four hours of general but ineffectual attacks against the Confederate line. At 1400, two regiments, the 3d Connecticut and 2nd Maine, were ordered to advance and take an enemy battery. The battery retreated, but the militia could not advance further against the combined artillery and infantry fire. The brigade was then sent on a flanking movement around the Confederate positions. While on the move, they discovered the rest of the Union army to be in retreat. At that moment Keyes's was the only well-organized brigade on the same side of Bull Run as the Confederates. A battalion of the Maine forces was then detached to help locate another brigade while the Connecticut regiments formed a brigade while fording the stream of Bull Run. They then turned and formed a line of companies. These 2500 tired rain and sweat soaked Connecticut and Maine volunteers then held their line while 800 Confederate cavalry charged. Holding their fire until the horsemen were within 100 yards of their line, the militia opened fire and repulsed the attack, taking six prisoners in the process. Thus, the 3d Connecticut was able to proudly return to Washington not only in good order but with prisoners unlike the majority of the Regular and volunteer forces on the field that day.

This unit continued to serve. It spent World War I as a coastal defense unit and World War II as a Field Artillery Headquarters Battery fighting its way across Europe. In 1959 it became Company B, 162 Transportation Battalion. In 1972 it became Detachment 1, 1109th Transportation Company.

Then, Connecticut had to reorganize a higher echelon unit, eliminating a number of these small units. This historic, but non-lineage bearing detachment was slated for extinction. Fortunately, this proposed action was noticed in the National Guard Bureau and the Organizational History Branch of the Center of Military History was called upon for advice. This small detachment with a 204 year history of service and bravery is now being consolidated with another unit entitled to Lineage and Honors and so its heritage will live on.

But these reorganizations are not always caught in time. Only the states and territories, knowing their own histories, can be the true guardians of their past.

—Martin K. Gordon

In one of its many reorganizations, the Norwich Light Infantry was Headquarters Battery, 1st Battalion, 192d Field Artillery, administering this unit as it showed off during the Louisiana maneuvers just before World War II.

Fort Barton, where the Connecticut and Rhode Island Militia mustered in summer 1777, survives today as an historic fort with trees now standing where once soldiers stood.

THE SAGA OF THE NORWICH LIGHT INFANTRY:

ONLY YOU CAN SAVE YOUR HISTORY

BIBLIOGRAPHY

Davis, William C. *Battle at Bull Run: A History of the First Major Campaign of the Civil War.* New York: Doubleday & Co., Inc., 1977.

Hinman, Royal Ralph. *A Historical Collection from Official Records, Files, &c., of the Part Sustained by Connecticut, during the War of the Revolution With an Appendix, Containing Important Letters, Depositions, &c., Written During the War.* Hartford: E. Gleason, 1842.

Holt, James W., Jr. *Fort Barton: Authentic Revolutionary War Redoubt and Nature Walk.* Tiverton, RI: Town Council, n.d.

    A descriptive brochure.

Niven, John. *Connecticut for the Union: The Role of the State in the Civil War.* New Haven: Yale Univ. Press, 1965.

Peckham, Howard H., ed. *The Toll of Independence: Engagements & Battle Casualties of the American Revolution.* Chicago: Univ. of Chicago Press, 1974.

U. S. Army. Center of Military History. Organizational History Branch. "Unit File: 1109th Transportation Company and its detachment."

POSTSCRIPT

The consolidation discussed at the end of the essay took place 1 August 1979 with the Headquarters and Headquarters Detachment of the 192d Engineer Battalion.

This essay originally appeared in the November 1979 *Push Pin Post*. It was written as the consolidation was starting.

The Richmond Light Infantry Blues

The Blues, parading in Richmond in 1954, are wearing their dress uniform which is practically unchanged from their uniform of the late 1830s.

National Guard units have meant several things to their communities. In the nineteenth century they were not only military but also social and political organizations. This historic Richmond, Virginia unit, now Troop E, 183d Cavalry (assigned to the 116th Infantry Brigade), VAARNG, exemplifies these strands of the militia tradition.

Eight years after Richmond was incorporated as a city, on 10 May 1789, a group of volunteers organized the Richmond Light Infantry choosing scarlet uniforms with black or white trimmings. That insensitivity to the remaining popular hostility towards anything resembling the British "redcoats" hurt recruiting and the unit nearly died out before it changed its uniforms to the popular blue trimmed with white in 1793. The Light Infantry soon acquired the nickname of "Blues," and eventually that became part of the official designation of the unit.

The social aspect of the company was shown in the requirement that, except in periods of actual war, an applicant for membership had to be passed on by the Board of Sergeants and then elected by the membership.

The political concerns of these citizen soldiers reached an unusual degree of intensity in the closing years of President John Adams' administration at the end of the 1700s. The officers and a number of the men, all Federalists, stayed with the Blues, while the rest of the unit split off and formed the Republican Blues in support of the new political party led by Thomas Jefferson. July, 1807 both companies were called to active duty and sent to Norfolk. The threatened invasion by the British Navy failed to materialize and the units were released from service after 20 days. Eventually political sentiments moderated and the Republican Blues disbanded. The Light Infantry Blues were able to continue their existence.

The Blues were called up several times during the War of 1812 but never actually engaged in combat with the British. The martial spirit of the citizens declined during the peaceful bustling years of the 1820s and the Blues spoke out against that trend, "in our opinion the safety of our city loudly calls for some armed, disciplined active force, which may at all times be ready to act under the control of the civil authorities when occasion requires." That was, of course, in the days of the beginnings of police forces.

This company was not called up for the War with Mexico but the years before the Civil War were not uneventful. It was activated several times because of fears of slave uprisings. Fulfilling the customary ceremonial role of the militia, the Blues acted as escorts to visiting dignitaries such as Lafayette and Presidents Van Buren, Polk, and Taylor. Political discussions again became lively at their meetings, but the citizen-soldiers this time felt that unity was more important than politics.

The Richmond Light Infantry Blues fought in the Civil War. Two of its captains were killed in that struggle and only 16 members were left in the company when Lee surrendered it along with the rest of his tired army at Appomattox Courthouse.

The rancor of the War healed and the Blues both hosted visiting Northern units and in turn visited the North. Two companies strong, it participated in the Spanish American War, serving in the Army of Cuban Occupation in Havana for three months.

Service in the World Wars has highlighted the command's activities in this century. Today, the Richmond Light Infantry Blues are still ready to serve at home or abroad wherever needed.

—Martin K. Gordon

THE RICHMOND LIGHT INFANTRY BLUES
BIBLIOGRAPHY

Angle, B. Bart, 1st Sgt. "Richmond Light Infantry Blues Observe 172d Anniversary." *Military Collector & Historian* 13 (Summer 1961): 63-64.

Cutchins, John A. *A Famous Command: The Richmond Light Infantry Blues*. Richmond: Garrett & Massie, Publishers, 1934.

"Life Goes Away to Camp with the Richmond Blues: Famed Virginia Battalion Begins Year's Army Training." *Life Magazine* (April 21, 1941): 112-113, 114, 117.

ERRATUM

The designation of the Richmond Light Infantry Blues in the first paragraph should read Troop C, not Troop E.

This essay originally appeared in the January 1977 *Push Pin Post*.

"Remember the Alamo"—Motto of the 141st Infantry

The military heritage of the citizen-soldiers of Texas is older than the formal history of their organized National Guard. The Washington Guards of Washington-on-the Brazos formed in 1836, Mirabeau Buonoparte Lamar's Laredo Guards of the 1846-1848 wars, the Grimes County Greys, the Texas Invincibles, the Lone Star Guards, and the Rifles of Navarro, all of the Civil War, exemplify that tradition. Those last named independent companies were, of course, part of John Bell Hood's Texas Brigade, the Texan component of Lee's Army of Northern Virginia. With the 14 battle honors those citizen soldiers won in four years of practically continuous combat, the pre-National Guard Texas militia established a high standard of conduct.

In the winter of 1870 the Texas militia was revived as State Guards. In 1878 the designation was changed to Texas Volunteers. The modern history of the Texas National Guard, and integral to it, the history of the 141st Infantry, dates from 6 April 1880. That date marks the beginnings of a permanent regimental structuring of the many independent companies, each based in its locality, which had previously existed. In 1903 the Texas Volunteer Guards formally became the Texas National Guard. The oldest company-sized unit in the current 141st, is Headquarters Company of the 1st Battalion, which was activated in 1912.

The 2d Infantry, Texas National Guard was activated in May 1916 for service on the Mexican Border. Concentrated at Fort Sam Houston, its mobilization point, the regiment immediately began a training program. On 27 May, units of the 2d Infantry began taking up positions on the border with Mexico.

President Woodrow Wilson asked Congress for a declaration of war against Germany 2 April 1917. Four days later Congress declared the country to be at war. The 1st Infantry was reactivated and also called into federal service. The regiments proceeded to Camp Bowie, Fort Worth, where in September they were consolidated under the wartime numbering scheme of the War Department to form the 141st Infantry, 36th Division.

By 27 July of the following year the 36th Division headquarters were established near Bar sur Aube, France. The Texans had arrived at the war. The 36th became one of ten divisions Pershing lent the French Fourth Army during the great Meuse–Argonne offensive which helped end the war. On 8 October the 141st, brigaded with the 142d, attacked in its first full scale major fight of the war. The two regiments suffered 1287 officers and men killed or wounded that day. The regiments stayed in contact with the enemy for two days. They later returned to the attack and so were in the front lines at the end of the war that November. Early in the summer of 1919 the regiments returned to the United States.

After years of routine peacetime training and inspection, the 141st Infantry was inducted into federal service, along with the entire 36th Division, on 25 November 1940. The Division landed in Oran, Algeria in the Spring of 1943. There, the Division was held in reserve and underwent further training. That training was to prove its value when the 141st hit the beach at Salerno, Italy, 9 September 1943. The 141st, under heavy German fire, took severe losses. The men were able to organize themselves ashore in spite of those casualties. The regiment's 3d Battalion won its Presidential Unit Citation for its actions during that amphibious assault.

That winter, 20 January 1944, at the Rapido River, below Rome, the 141st engaged in a bloody assault reminiscent of the Texan charge at Gettysburg. Thrown back by the well-entrenched enemy after two days of continuous fighting, the regiment was nearly destroyed. Reconstituted, it was able to participate in the liberation of Rome.

The regiment fought its way through the landings in Southern France where the 1st Battalion earned its Presidential Unit Citation. The "First Texas," as the regiment is nicknamed, raced the Germans across France fighting and capturing numbers of them. The German Nineteenth Army stood and fought west of the Rhine at Colmar. In the assaults upon that desperate force the 2d Battalion earned its Presidential Unit Citation. The Guardsmen went on to fight in the Battles of the Ardennes and the Rhineland before participating in the occupation of Austria. By the summer of 1945, the war was over and the 141st was on its way home. Once again the Texan citizen-soldiers had served their country well.

Martin K. Gordon

National Archives

Enlisted personnel of Headquarters Company, 141st Infantry, with the following officers: Capt W. C. Torrance, 1stLt H. H. Johnson, and 2dLt H. Mulhauser. In contrast with the combat actions narrated in the text, this photograph serves as a reminder that the service of the military goes beyond those moments spent in action against the enemy. Taken at Chaurce, Aube, France, 23 February 1919.

"REMEMBER THE ALAMO"--MOTTO OF THE 141st INFANTRY

BIBLIOGRAPHY

Henderson, Harry McC. *History of the 141st Infantry, 36th Infantry Division, Texas National Guard.* San Antonio: Press of the Naylor Company, 1950.

Simpson, Harold B., Col., ed. *Soldiers of Texas.* Waco: Texian Press, 1973.

Starr, Chester G. *From Salerno to the Alps.* Washington: Infantry Journal Press, 1948.

U. S. Army. Center of Military History. Organizational History Branch. "Unit File: 141st Infantry."

This essay originally appeared in the April 1977 *Push Pin Post*.

Pennsylvania's 28th Infantry Division: The Bloody Bucket

BEGINNINGS

Pennsylvania was going through exciting times 100 years ago. In addition to maintaining order in a time of riots, John F. Hartranft, the energetic governor, revised the state constitution, saw the state through the national centennial celebration in Philadelphia in 1876, started new programs, increased the state's role as a regulator, and reorganized the National Guard into the first modern NG division: the 28th.

The work of Hartranft and the state legislature began in June 1878 when the 21 divisional headquarters in the state were deactivated. The remaining regiments, battalions, and companies were then under direct state supervision. The new governor, Henry M. Hoyt, on March 12, 1879 activated Headquarters, Division of the National Guard of Pennsylvania, at Philadelphia with Hartranft as its first commanding

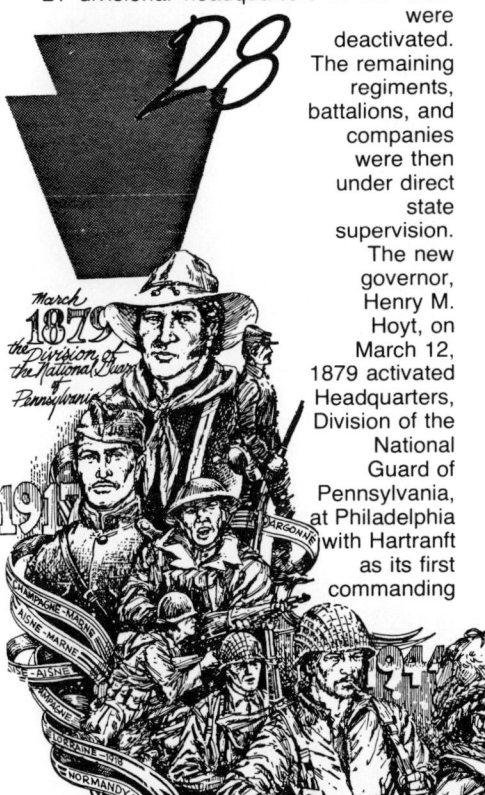

officer. He held the rank of Major General, which had been his rank at the end of the Civil War in 1865. Hartranft then reorganized his forces into five brigades, 16 regiments, and three battalions of infantry, five cavalry companies, and four artillery batteries. Some of those units had lineages dating back to Revolutionary War service.

AT TEN YEARS

May 31, 1889, the South Fork Dam below the Conemaugh River Reservoir broke and flooded Johnstown, Pennsylvania. At first city officials refused aid as unnecessary from the Washington Infantry and Battery "B" that had rushed to the site from Pittsburgh. They soon changed their minds and Pittsburgh's 14th Regiment and Johnstown's Company "H" were also called up. Over 500 Guardsmen were on duty at the peak of the relief effort. As one observer reported:

The soldiers come, but not on carnage bent—
Theirs is a noble, generous intent;
The guards are placed, heard is the sentry's tramp
The wasted district has been made a camp.

MOBILIZATIONS

The call for volunteers for Spanish-American War service only asked the states to send regiments or other units of lower levels. Thus, although 12,315 Pennsylvania Guardsmen mobilized for that war, their division did not.

It was different June 29, 1916, when the 7th Division, PANG, as it was known, was mustered into federal service at Mount Gretna for duty on the Mexican border. The division was mustered out February 23, 1917 at Philadelphia.

THE FIRST WORLD WAR

The division was ordered into federal service July 15, 1917 and reorganized September 1 at Camp Hancock, Georgia, where it was redesignated the 28th Division. It went overseas in May and June 1918 in time to participate in six major campaigns: Champane-Marne, Aisne-Marne, Oise-Aisne, Meuse-Argonne, Champagne 1918 and Lorraine 1918. Its units bore the brunt of the 1918 German last offensive and in turn participated in the last great Allied offensive assaulting the Argonne Forest. The division took 921 prisoners and suffered 13,980 casualties in the war. After occupation duty, it returned home in the spring of 1919.

THE SECOND WORLD WAR

Inducted into federal service in February 1941 and trained in England, the 28th landed in Normandy, France July 22, 1944. The Germans nicknamed the division, "the bloody bucket," after its red keystone insignia, during that summer's fighting through the hedgerows that the enemy were using as strong defensive lines. By August 20, the division was rolling across France attempting to stop and capture the fleeing Germans. On August 29, the division paraded through Paris and continued its advance through Luxembourg to Germany, averaging 17 miles a day.

The division passed within 25 miles of a memorial to its World War I service as it advanced from Paris to Germany. On November 2, 1944 the Keystoners joined the bloody battle for Hurtgen Forest with its continuous attacks and counterattacks. After completing that mission it was given a 25 mile sector to hold. The German surprise attack that December struck the sector with five refitted divisions. As the 28th held, four more German divisions were thrown against it in that part of the Battle of the Bulge. The 28th fought in place and threw the German time table completely off schedule. The division went on to participate in the reduction of German positions in Colmar, France and along the Rhine. After 196 days in combat, taking 8,661 prisoners, and suffering 24,840 casualties, it was sent home July 1945 and inactivated that December.

AFTER THE WAR

The 28th was the first NG division to gain federal recognition after the war, November 20, 1946. It was again ordered into active federal service September 5, 1950 and was sent to Southern Germany in November 1951 as NATO reinforcements during the Korean War. Released from federal service 25 years ago in June 1954, the 28th is currently preparing to celebrate its centennial.

THE CENTENNIAL CELEBRATION

The division is planning many activities to commemorate its 100th year. Details are available from Col. Uzal W. Ent, HQ, 28th Infantry Division, Bldg. No. 1, Harrisburg Military Post, 14th and Calder Streets, Harrisburg, PA 17103 (717-787-6705).

—Martin K. Gordon

PENNSYLVANIA'S 28th INFANTRY DIVISION: THE BLOODY BUCKET
BIBLIOGRAPHY

Dictionary of American Biography, vol. 8, "Hartranft, John F." by Witt Bowden.

Hill, Jim Dan. *The Minute Man in Peace and War: A History of the National Guard*. Harrisburg, PA: Stackpole Co., 1964.

McCullough, David G. *The Johnstown Flood*. New York: Simon and Schuster, 1968.

McLaurin, J. J. *The Story of Johnstown: Its Early Settlement, Rise and Progress, Industrial Growth, and Appalling Flood on May 31st 1889*. Harrisburg: James M. Place, Publisher, 1890.

    The source of the quotation about the Guard at the Johnstown Flood used in this essay.

Ohl, John K. "The Keystone Division in the Great War." *Prologue: The Journal of the National Archives* 10 (Summer 1978): 83-99.

U. S. Army. Center of Military History. Organizational History Branch. "Unit Files: 28th Infantry Division, subordinate commands."

    The principal source for this essay.

This essay originally appeared in the March 1979 *Push Pin Post*.

Thomas Jefferson and the Militia

Thomas Jefferson always preferred the militia to the regular Army. As he wrote during his first campaign for the presidency in 1799, "I am for relying, for internal defense, on our militia solely, till actual invasion, and for such a naval force only as may protect our coasts and harbors... and not for a standing army in time of peace, which may overawe the public sentiment." Jefferson was in favor of the militia and opposed to a large regular force for two reasons. Cost was one factor, while fear of a politicized army was an equally important consideration. Jeffersonian Republicans had been frozen out of the officer corps of the additional forces authorized by Congress during the war scare of 1798.

Jefferson evolved a three part military policy. The Army was to be kept just large enough for frontier duty and to provide for training artillerists and engineers. The Navy was to be restricted as much as possible to a coastal defense role, and reliance was to be placed on the militia in times of national emergency. The United States Military Academy at West Point was founded in this era to provide the trained specialists the Army needed, but also with the understanding that any graduates not joining the Army would be expected to return to their home areas, join the militia, and contribute their skills to that force.

THE JEFFERSONIAN YEARS

In Jefferson's first inaugural address, March 4, 1801, he argued that the United States had, "the strongest government on earth... the only one where every man, at the call of the law, would fly to the standard of the law, and would meet invasions of the public order as his own personal concern." He called a well-disciplined militia, "our best reliance in peace and for the first moments of war, till regulars may relieve them." Jefferson and Congress translated their belief in the citizen-soldier into legislation.

ACTION

Congress adopted legislation March 1803 which required the adjutant general of each state to file a report of the strength and equipment of his militia with the Secretary of War. The states reacted inconsistently to this early Federal paperwork requirement. Reporting was good until after the War of 1812 and sporadic between 1815 and 1862 when this requirement was dropped as the new more efficient National Guard began to evolve. Massachusetts led the states reporting in 96% of the years. Reporting varied wildly between the other states with Virginia reporting in 87% of the years, Maryland in 26% and Delaware in only 7% of the years.

With the partial failure of this legislation and the recurring war scares of the early 1800s in mind, Congress, with Jefferson's support, passed the April 1808 Act for Arming the Militia. This legislation, the first and for a long time the only federal grant-in-aid to the states was designed to improve both the reporting and the equipment of the militia. The act appropriated $200,000 per year to be divided among the states for weapons and equipment in proportion to the strengths reported in the annual returns. In practice, this act helped the regulars along with the militia. The Army used the money to buy new weapons and equipment for itself, then released the replaced items to the states. They did not receive the cash, nor did the states respond much better with this inducement.

Even in the war year of 1813, the Secretary of War was forced to use returns up to three years out of date. That was the era of the enrolled or compulsory militia when most able-bodied white males were considered part of the militia. Using that population group as the basis for their figures, the state and territorial adjutants general reported in 1809–1812 that a total of 719,449 men were available for compulsory militia duty. (Louisiana might have included its volunteer black militia in its reported totals.) Pennsylvania, with an up to date report, counted 99,414 men available for militia duty. New York claimed the next largest militia with 98,606 men. Obviously, these figures, broken into types of units and amounts of equipment gave the president and Congress some useful information, but these reports can be considered more as studies on draft eligibility than a record of units immediately available for service.

SYMBOLS

Jefferson was also aware of the symbolic importance of his work as the third president of a new republic. Because of the unique nature of federal control over the District of Columbia, Jefferson was also the commander-in-chief of its militia. In October 1802, Jefferson formally reviewed a muster of the D.C. Militia in civilian dress. The local conservative newspaper attacked him for insulting the militia by not appearing in uniform as commander of that force. The Jeffersonian press replied that the President had not worn a uniform because the civilian power is superior to the military power, and the president was the civilian commander of the military power. Jefferson said the same thing in June 1804 when he took his guest, the European scientist Baron Alexander von Humboldt to see a company-level D.C. Militia muster. The European aristocrat asked why Jefferson was not in uniform, and Jefferson reminded him of the nature of civilian control of the military in the United States.

Thus, it can be demonstrated that President Thomas Jefferson and his Congresses worked hard to improve the military force in which they believed—the American citizen-soldier.

—Martin K. Gordon

Thomas Jefferson (Courtesy of the Library of Congress)

THOMAS JEFFERSON AND THE MILITIA
BIBLIOGRAPHY

Gordon, Martin K. "The District of Columbia Militia, 1790-1815." Ph. D. dissertation, The George Washington University, 1975.

Jefferson, Thomas. Inaugural Addresses.

    Any edition can be used.

Jacobs, James R. The Beginning of the U.S. Army, 1783-1812. Princeton: Princeton Univ. Press, 1947.

Miller, John C. The Federalist Era. The New American Nation Series. New York: Harper & Row, Pubs., Harper Torchbooks, 1963.

Padover, Saul K., ed. Thomas Jefferson on Democracy. New York: New American Library, Mentor Books, 1946.

Riker, William H. Soldiers of the States: The Role of the National Guard in American Democracy. Washington: Public Affairs Press, 1957.

This essay originally appeared in the July 1979 Push Pin Post.

Edgar Allan Poe: Poet, Author and Sometime Militiaman

Edgar Allan Poe, the great American author and poet, began his military career while a school boy in Richmond, Virginia. He joined the Junior Morgan Riflemen later the Richmond Junior Volunteers, a school boy unit, in the Autumn of 1824 at the age of 15. Organized to help welcome the aged Revolutionary War hero, the Marquis de Lafayette to Richmond during his tour of the United States, this company, like many other militia companies, also served as a home guard force for the city. The state kept a portion of the regiment of State Guards on duty at all times at the penitentiary in case of civil disorder. When that regiment was sent out of town to help welcome Lafayette, several new units were then organized to stand by in the city until the regular guard force could return. Among those units which also helped welcome the Marquis were the Junior Riflemen. Armed with the same weapons that the adult militia carried, the Junior Morgan Riflemen wore a uniform of the distinctive, fringed hunting shirts of the frontier riflemen.

Poe served as lieutenant of the company. His unit paraded in the welcoming festivities and later had the honor of serving as Lafayette's personal escort while he was in Richmond. The boys enjoyed the ceremonial life of a militia unit in that era and asked the governor of the state if they could keep their arms after Lafayette left and continue to drill. The governor's reply is unknown.

Poe soon left Richmond to enroll at the University of Virginia where he was active in the student militia company. Poe dropped out of college and joined the regular army where he quickly rose to the rank of sergeant-major. He then entered the United States Military Academy at West Point. He finally settled for the life of a literary man after sampling all the military styles his country had to offer in the 1820s and 1830s.

Lafayette inspecting the Junior Morgan Riflemen. Drawing by Sally Goyea

The Star-Spangled Patriot

Everyone knows that Francis Scott Key wrote the "Star-Spangled Banner," but who, trivia fans, originated the custom of standing while the National Anthem is played. You guessed right. It was a Guardsman, Brigadier General Rossell Galbraith O'Brian from the state of Washington. General O'Brian, who organized the first Washington National Guard Company, presented a resolution to the two dozen members of the Commandery of the Loyal Legion that "whenever the music of the 'Star-Spangled Banner' shall be played, every member of the Loyal Legion of the State of Washington, if present, shall rise to his feet and uncover..." The resolution was approved and a new tradition had begun. General O'Brian was born in Ireland, but came to the United States when he was four. He served as a lieutenant in the Civil War and moved to Washington in 1870. There he served in a variety of positions including assistant assessor of Internal Revenue, clerk of the U.S. Supreme Court and District Court and served nine consecutive years on the Olympia City Council and one term as Mayor of the city. He moved to California just after the turn of the century and died in 1914.

copyright 1975, *The American Legion Magazine*. Reprinted by permission.

Edgar Allan Poe
This portrait by Thomas C. Corner was painted in 1934 from the best extant likeness of Poe. Courtesy of the Enoch Pratt Free Library, Baltimore, Md.

Story by Martin Gordon

EDGAR ALLAN POE: POET, AUTHOR AND SOMETIME MILITIAMAN

BIBLIOGRAPHY

Allen, Hervey. <u>Israfel: The Life and Times of Edgar Allan Poe</u>.
New York: Rinehart and Company, Inc., 1949.

Helfers, Melvin C. "The Military Career of Edgar Allan Poe."
M. A. thesis, Duke University, 1949.

Ostrom, John Ward, ed., <u>The Letters of Edgar Allan Poe</u>. 2 vols.
New York: Gordian Press, Inc., 1966.

Quinn, Arthur H. <u>Edgar Allan Poe: A Critical Biography</u>.
New York: D. Appleton-Century Co., 1941.

Russel, J. Thomas. <u>Edgar Allan Poe: The Army Years</u>.
USMA Library Bulletin No. 10. West Point: United States
Military Academy, 1972.

Stanard, Mary Newton. <u>Richmond: Its People and Its Story</u>.
Philadelphia: J. B. Lippincott Co., 1923.

Discusses Lafayette's visit to Richmond.

This essay originally appeared in the February 1976 <u>Push Pin Post</u>.

THE PRESIDENT HAD BEEN IN THE MILITIA

There was a pattern to the way politicians involved themselves in the work of the citizen-soldier in the last century. At the local level, politicians often joined or even organized militia companies in order to have a base for their operations. Companies of one religious creed, or one ethnic group, or one party or even one faction of a party were common throughout the militia at least until the beginnings of the modern National Guard in the 1870s to 1890s time period.

At the state level, governors often rewarded their faithful supporters with commissions on their military staffs. Those commissions were based on the same authority as that used by some governors today when they commission a prominent citizen as an honorary officer of the state military forces. The nineteenth century military staffs, usually unpaid, served for the political connections it gave them and for the fun of attending the governor in full dress uniform upon the annual review of the militia or other state occasions.

This was the background to President Chester A. Arthur's Civil War era service in the militia, later National Guard, of the state of New York. Arthur had been active in New York City and state politics while he worked as an attorney in the City in the mid-1850s. On Feb. 3, 1858, he was commissioned judge advocate of the state's Second Brigade, a typical position for a young attorney interested in both gaining clients and forging political connections. Through those connections, Republican Governor Edwin D. Morgan was influenced to appoint Arthur to his staff. Arthur and Morgan had not met before the appointment but they soon became friends.

On Jan., 1861, Morgan commissioned Arthur engineer-in-chief of the state militia with the rank of brigadier general. The Civil War started four months later. New York state appropriated $3,000,000 to arm and equip up to 30,000 soldiers and another half-million dollars for the defense of the state. Arthur's orders to active duty with the rest of the state staff arrived the day after the Confederacy occupied Fort Sumter.

General Arthur occupied a major role in bringing the full weight of the North's militia into action. He represented the Quartermaster General's office in New York City. Without prior training or experience, he had to help feed, house, clothe, and equip the men of the regiments not only from New York City and state, but also those from the New England states who passed through his city on their way to the army. As Arthur soon began to prove his administrative abilities, Governor Morgan depended more on his judgment and soon gave him the additional title of Acting Assistant Quartermaster General. Arthur handled everything from auditing to underwear as the state sent 38 of its regiments south into action by the middle of July 1861. Arthur worked as hard as his superior, Governor Morgan, and was personally and politically acceptable to him. On Feb. 10, 1862, Morgan appointed Arthur Inspector General of the state's forces and six months later, July 10, Arthur became the state's Quartermaster General.

Arthur's career in the NYNG lasted until the Democratic Party defeated Governor Morgan in the 1862 elections. That meant that Arthur and the rest of Morgan's military staff had to resign their commissions as of Jan., 1863, when the Republicans left office. Arthur returned to his law practice.

The future President's five years of active and inactive service in the militia was a reputation-making high-point in his career. He displayed basic leadership qualities in such areas as the ability to instill confidence in his subordinates, make quick decisions, and to competently handle crises. For example, he personally ripped the shoulder-straps from the uniform of a New York alderman, "Billy" Wilson who claimed the rank of colonel on the basis of a gang of hoodlums he had recruited as a regiment and then refused to discipline. There were other such incidents in those frantic times when anybody who could recruit soldiers could gain a commission as their officer.

Interestingly, both Arthur's and Morgan's administration of the war effort was honest and efficient. Later Arthur gained a reputation as a machine politician who used federal jobs as sources of political patronage and revenue. This reputation caused his removal as head of the New York Customhouse in the 1870s.

Elected Vice-President in 1880, he became President upon the death of President James A. Garfield, being sworn in on Sept. 20, 1881. Arthur then reverted to being the honest efficient administrator he had been when in uniform. The legislative foundations of a nonpartisan career civil service, and of the modern Navy were two of the reforms undertaken during his administration. Although our 21st President served as and used the title of "General," he never saw combat but instead exemplified the tradition of those who provide the materiel support necessary for the combat soldiers to do their job.

—Martin K. Gordon

Library of Congress
General Chester Alan Arthur in full military uniform, photographed c. 1862. He later became the 21st President of the United States.

THE PRESIDENT HAD BEEN IN THE MILITIA

BIBLIOGRAPHY

Dictionary of American Biography, vol 1. "Arthur, Chester Alan." by Frederic Logan Paxson.

Reeves, Thomas C. Gentleman Boss: The Life of Chester A. Arthur. New York: Alfred A, Knopf, 1975.

    Contains excellent footnote references to Arthur's military career.

This essay originally appeared in the January 1978 Push Pin Post.

CHARLES A. LINDBERGH: GUARDSMAN

Charles A. Lindbergh probably joined the National Guard because of the encouragement of his employer. Major William B. Robertson, the first commanding officer of Missouri's 35th Division Air Service, gave the young pilot a job testing planes and instructing students when Lindbergh arrived in St. Louis at the end of October 1925. Major Robertson had known Lindbergh since October 1923 when they had met at the International Air Races at St. Louis. While Lindbergh was hanging around the air field that fall of 1923, some National Guard pilots, probably World War I flying veterans, talked to him about joining the Army so that he could learn more about techniques and mechanics of flying than he could as a free-lance barnstormer. Marvin Northrop, of Northrop Aviation, also pointed out to Lindbergh that Army flying training made a good starting point for other things as it had for Northrop himself. Furthermore, Lindbergh wanted to fly the more powerful 400 horse power engines that the Army was using in their De Havilands. He was getting bored with barnstorming.

After the appropriate paperwork and examinations, Lindbergh joined the 15 March 1924 class of flying pilots at Brooks Field, San Antonio, Texas. A year later he was one of the 18 members of his entering class of 104 cadets to graduate. That same month, Lindbergh resigned from the Army and accepted a lieutenant's commission in the reserve corps. That October he arrived in St. Louis and went to work for Major Robertson. On 16 November 1925 Lindbergh enlisted as a private in the 110th Observation Squadron of the 35th Division Air Service. On 7 December, that same winter, he was commissioned a first lieutenant. Rising quickly, Lindbergh made captain on 13 July 1926. The only surviving record of his specific duties states that on 1 January 1927, he was assigned as flight commander, parachute officer, and pilot in the squadron.

That same January, Major C.R. Wassall, commanding the 35th Division Air Service, wrote in an official report, "I consider Captain Lindbergh one of the most efficient officers in the National Guard Air Corps." Lindbergh, in turn, wrote about his fellow Air Guardsmen, "The organization was composed mainly of pilots who had flown during the war, but after the Armistice had gone back to civilian life. Their only method of keeping in training was by flying National Guard planes in their spare moments and attending camp two weeks each year. Two nights and one day each week were devoted to military service by these officers and the enlisted men under them. Their pay was small and most of them lost more from neglect to their businesses than they received for their military services. The remuneration was hardly considered. However they joined the Guard for two reasons: 1st, because of the opportunity it offered to keep in flying training and 2nd, because they considered it a patriotic duty to keep fit for immediate service in case of national emergency. Appropriations were not large and often insufficient but, although at times it required part of the squadron's pay checks, the ships were kept in the air."

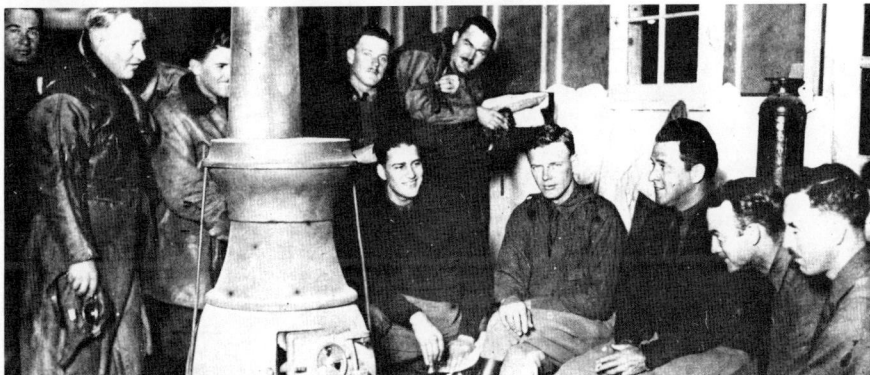

Charles A. Lindbergh at summer camp with his fellow Guardsmen.

Yale University Library

In the fall of 1926, Lindbergh became interested in trying for the $25,000 Raymond Orteig Prize for the first non-stop flight from New York to Paris. But he needed money and backers. Lindbergh thought about asking the Wright Aeronautical Corporation for money but all he had in the way of business clothes was a worn blue suit and his captain's uniform. As he later explained, "A captain's uniform is the only good suit I own, and one just doesn't wear an officer's uniform on personal business." Later during training, Lindbergh sought out the best dressed officer in the squadron and asked his advice on what to wear. Captain Littlefield recommended his tailor and a tailor-made suit for Lindbergh's business trips.

What followed is well-known history. On 20 February 1927, Captain Lindbergh obtained a four month's leave of absence from the Missouri Guard with permission to leave the state. On 20 May 1927, Lindbergh began his famous flight from Roosevelt Field, New York. When he landed 33½ hours later, Lindbergh was an international hero.

The Chief of the Militia Bureau and the Adjutant General of Missouri wanted to exploit this by having Lindbergh arrive back in the U.S. in his Missouri National Guard uniform. But the Secretary of War took advantage of the fact that Lindbergh also still held his commission in the Army Reserve and immediately promoted him to full colonel. The Army Air Corps then had a uniform made for Colonel Lindbergh from his measurements on file in the War Department and delivered to him while he was still at sea. Thus, Lindbergh would land as a colonel in the Air Reserve. The Wright Corporation's public relations man, Dick Blythe, talked Lindbergh into arriving in his blue suit instead because he had made the flight as a civilian and furthermore, Lindbergh might lose some of his popularity if he arrived in an Army Air Corps uniform. The regulars were able to remind the public of Lindbergh's reserve status, however, when Congress voted him the Medal of Honor as a Captain in the Army Air Corps Reserve. The Orteig Prize committee knew differently, though, when they voted the award to Captain Charles Lindbergh, "an officer of the Missouri National Guard."

Lindbergh kept renewing his leave of absence every four months until 2 June 1930 when he was transferred to the National Guard Reserve at his own request. The Missouri legislature promoted him to colonel in that reserve force. While in the NG Reserve, he helped his old unit with publicity and once, during national Air Corps maneuvers in 1931 led the participating 35th Division aviation units. When Congress replaced the National Guard Reserve with the Inactive National Guard in 1933, Colonel Lindbergh severed all connections with the Missouri National Guard.

—Martin K. Gordon
NGB–IC–77–57

CHARLES A. LINDBERGH: GUARDSMAN

BIBLIOGRAPHY

Davis, Kenneth S. The Hero: Charles A. Lindbergh and the American Dream. Garden City: Doubleday & Co., Inc., 1959.

"Lindbergh as a Guardsman." Quartermaster Review 14 (March-April 1935): 50-51, 76.

Lindbergh, Charles A. The Spirit of St. Louis. New York: Scribner, 1953.

_____. "We," The Famous Flier's own Story of his Life and Transatlantic Flight, together with His Views on the Future of Aviation. New York: G. P. Putnam's Sons, 1927.

Missouri Historical Society, St. Louis. Illustrations of Colonel Lindbergh's Decorations and some of his trophies. St. Louis: Missouri Historical Society, 1935.

Missouri. National Guard. Historical Annual, National Guard and Naval Militia of the State of Missouri. Baton Rouge: Army & Navy Pub. Co., 1939.

_____. History of the Missouri National Guard, Published by Authority of the Military Council, Missouri National Guard. n. p., n. pub, 1934.

Mosley, Leonard. Lindbergh: A Biography. Garden City: Doubleday & Co., Inc., 1976.

Ross, Walter S. The Last Hero: Charles A. Lindbergh. New York: Harper & Row, 1976.

Schiff, Judith A. "The Life and Letters of Charles A. Lindbergh: A Commemorative View." The Yale University Library Gazette (April 1977): 173-189.

U. S. Army. Center of Military History. Organizational History Branch. "Unit File: 35th Infantry Division."

The author wishes to acknowledge with gratitude the assistance of Captain Clyde Martin, Chief, Archives Branch, Missouri Adjutant General's Office.

ERRATUM

The credit line on the photograph should read: Charles A. Lindbergh Papers, Yale University Library.

This essay originally appeared in the November 1977 Push Pin Post.

The Bedford Flag

"By the rude bridge that arched the flood, Their flag to April's breeze unfurled, Here once the embattled farmers stood, And fired the shot heard round the world." Ralph Waldo Emerson wrote those lines in 1836 about a militia flag at the battle of Concord. The question is which flag?

There is today in the Bedford, Massachusetts Public Library, a flag which might have inspired Emerson. Originally painted in England in the mid-seventeenth century, that flag had been a cavalry standard of the Three County Troop organized in eastern Massachusetts in Essex, Suffolk, and Middlesex counties in 1659. The English flag of the early 1630s displayed the red cross of St. George, which was considered a Popish symbol by the Puritans of early New England. They preferred plain flags which included such proper symbolism as that shown on this flag, the arm and the sword reaching from the cloud implying victory through strength in "the arm of the Lord." That symbolism was popular in the 1600s and was used by units of the New Model Army of Cromwell's revolutionary England. Its Latin motto, "Conquer or Die," also reflects the tendency towards the use of mottos by the new military units of that century.

Legend tells that Nathaniel Page, the third generation of his family to be active in the local militia, took it from his closet when he was called out on the morning of April 19, 1775 for the battle of Concord. His ancestors, so the story goes, had brought the flag with them from England in 1687. Later that day, he put down the flag to help tend the dead and wounded. After rescuing the flag from a group of children playing with it, he took it home again. It was brought out again for the centennial commemoration of the battle of Concord in 1875 and was donated to the town of Bedford in 1885.

Photo courtesy of the Bedford Free Public Library where the Bedford Flag now reposes.

While the Bedford Flag is certainly an historic militia flag, reflecting the spirit of the colonial citizen-soldiers, the stories of its use at Concord must be considered legendary rather than historic. The first claim that George Washington and representatives of the Continental Congress called on Betsy Ross to ask her to manufacture the first national flag was made in 1870, just before the centennial of the United States. So too, the first claim that the Bedford Flag was at the first day of the American Revolution at Concord was made in April 1875 during the centennial commemoration of that battle. The Sudbury militia also claim to have carried a flag that fateful day, and it is impossible to determine the truth of the claims made for the Bedford Flag.

What is true is that the Bedford Flag stands as a treasured piece of National Guard and American history. It shows the continuous determination of the militia through the centuries to defend their towns under symbols of their own choosing.

—Martin K. Gordon

THE BEDFORD FLAG

BIBLIOGRAPHY

Campbell, Gordon, Vice-Adm., and Evans, I. O. *The Book of Flags*.
    London: Oxford University Press, 1966.

Smith, Whitney. "The Bedford Flag." *The Flag Bulletin* 10
    (Spring-Summer 1971): 46-54. Also titled *Report of the
    Third International Congress of Vexillology*.

    An especially useful article.

_____. *Flags Through the Ages and Across the World*.
    New York: McGraw-Hill Book Company, 1975.

AN ADDITIONAL SOURCE

Chester, Joseph L. "The Standard of the Three County Troop."
    New England Historical and Genealogical Register
    25 (April 1871): 138-140.

This essay originally appeared in the November 1976 *Push Pin Post*.

THE MILITIA FLAG THAT HELPED CATCH AN ASSASSIN

> This article is the first in a series that will highlight some of the lesser known episodes and personalities in the history of the National Guard. We hope you will enjoy them.

John Wilkes Booth, as it is well known, broke into the Ford's Theater presidential box, shot President Abraham Lincoln and escaped by vaulting over the rail of the box onto the stage and running out of the building. But few people know the crucial role played by the militia in catching Booth. For while vaulting out of the box, the assassin caught his spur in the flag of the Treasury Guards, a home guard militia regiment, and broke a bone in his ankle when he landed. The flag was draped in the middle of the decorations in front of the presidential box. The broken bone was to lead to Booth's eventual capture.

President Lincoln let it be known that he would make one of his regular trips to Ford's Theatre April 14, 1865. John T. Ford, the theatre's owner, needed decorations for the presidential box. The Treasury Guards rented their national and regimental colors to the proprietor to help him out for the night. The regiment itself did not escort the President although the presence of its colors gave rise to that rumor.

The regiment, composed of the able-bodied male clerks of the Treasury Department, drilled one hour a day during their normal working hours. There had been previous attempts to organize Treasury workers for military duty during the Civil War but none had endured. Then, Jubal Early's rapidly-executed and nearly successful attack on Washington, D.C. gave a new impetus to home guard defense organizations while the volunteer militia was away at war. The men wore the basic uniform of light blue infantry trousers, dark blue 4-button jackets, and for head dress fatigue caps bearing the brass regimental insignia. The women clerks of the Department participated by presenting their male colleagues with two flags, the national colors and a regimental flag. That regimental flag, borne in parades, was six by six and one-half feet. It still carries the tear caused by the spur of John Wilkes Booth in its upper right edge.

Story by Martin Gordon

The box where the Lincoln assassination took place. The Treasury Guards' Regimental flag is in the center.
Photo courtesy of National Park Service.

Ford's Theater in April of 1865. Photo courtesy of National Park Service.

THE MILITIA FLAG THAT HELPED CATCH AN ASSASSIN

BIBLIOGRAPHY

Buckingham, J. E., Sr. <u>Reminiscences and Souvenirs of The Assassination of Abraham Lincoln</u>. Washington: Press of Rufus H. Darby, 1894.

    See Chapter IX, "A Building That Has A Tragic History."

Genns, Whitney T. "The Flag That Tripped Booth." <u>The Sunday Star</u> (Washington, DC), 3 June 1934, p. 11.

Miller, Robert L. "U. S. Treasury Guards." <u>Military Collector & Historian</u> 15 (Spring 1963): 22-23.

Smith, James B., Jr. "Conservation of a Century-Old Painted Flag." <u>Military Collector & Historian</u> 22 (Winter 1970): 113-118.

U. S., Department of The Interior., National Park Service., National Capital Region, Lincoln Museum. "Museum Catalogue Record." Catalogue No. 22, Accession No. 65.

    Contains background information on both the flag and the Treasury Guards.

This essay originally appeared in the January 1976 <u>Push Pin Post</u>.

It's Your History Too

The time has arrived, in this series of essays, to talk about you and the preservation of the heritage of the National Guard. The author of this series cannot do it alone, neither can any of the Washington-based military history agencies.

One year ago this month two historic National Guard sites, the State Armory, Springfield, Massachusetts and the Blues Armory, Richmond, Virginia were placed on the National Register of Historic Places. (The Richmond Blues were discussed in this column in January 1977.) The Springfield Armory was built in 1895 as that city's first building for the local militia. The Blues building, dating from 1910, is used by both military groups and commercial interests. Yet those buildings are but two samples of the different architectural styles that are the physical reminders of the history of the Guard that exist throughout the country.

Not all Guard armories, encampment sites, fortifications, and other similar places are of sufficient merit to be entered in the National Register. But no one will ever know their value unless you take an interest. Local and state officials had to cooperatively initiate the paperwork for the recognition granted the Springfield and Richmond sites. All sites require the same local initiative. There are also lesser degrees of federal recognition, all of which must be worked out between the initiators and the State Historic Preservation Officer.

The militia is much older than the armory system. Through the early 1800s, the state or other appropriate authority issued arms as available and as required directly to the individual and then had to try and get them back at demobilization. For a while, the company and regimental commanders were required to give personal bond for the weapons issued to their troops. During this period the company commanders experimented with keeping all of their men's weapons in their own homes. This system only pleased those legendary company commanders who were also tavern keepers. The men had an added encouragement to stop off for a quick drink or two after their drill if it would also save them a trip to turn in their muskets or rifles. Sometime before the Civil War, the various militias began to erect or rent armories where their weapons could be kept and where they could drill and practice firing exercises all year around.

Many of the older armories surviving today were built between the 1870s and World War I. Many of them look like castles and they do so for an obvious reason. In that age of urban turmoil, as state police forces also under state control were just beginning to be developed, those armories were centers of urban stability. They were used not only in a martial sense of weapons storage, but also for social events and as centers of relief activities during local emergencies.

Now, as the pressure to tear down and build anew seems to go on and on, it is important that you document the existence of those physical touchstones with earlier Guardsmen.

Photographs, newspaper clippings, paintings and other artwork, and oral history tapes of local oldtimers can all contribute to an awareness of your local heritage. Sometimes, the building itself cannot or should not be preserved. Its memory can be preserved, however.

There are three good starting places for the local unit historian or history buff. The somewhat misnamed *Guide to U. S. Army Museums and Historic Sites*, published by the Center of Military History, Department of the Army, Washington, contains more than is indicated in the title. It also lists ARNG museums and private, state, and municipal military museums. Helpful to the beginning unit historian is its section, "Sources of Information on Military History." A list of State Historic Preservation Officers and further specific information can be found in Army TM 5-801-1 of November 1975, *Historic Preservation Administrative Procedures*.

The Council on Abandoned Military Posts (CAMP) is a private nonprofit organization composed of members from all states, men and women, young and old, military, Guard, reserve and regular, and civilians, whose concern is the preservation of those places where the military has served the country in the past. CAMP offers a means of both preserving and publicizing your particular historic site through its newsletter and periodical publication program. CAMP can also refer your inquiries to specialists or preservation enthusiasts in your area who might be able to assist in your research work. Information and membership materials can be obtained from the National Secretary, P. O. Box 171, Arlington, VA 22210.

After all, it's your history too.

—Martin K. Gordon

National Register of Historic Places

Not to be confused with the United States Arsenal in Springfield, this historic building was Springfield's first building erected for the local volunteer militia. Over a year in construction, this armory was completed in 1895.

IT'S YOUR HISTORY TOO

BIBLIOGRAPHY

Cary, Norman M., Jr. <u>Guide to U. S. Army Museums and Historic Sites</u>. A Bicentennial Publication of the United States Army Center of Military History. Washington: Government Printing Office, 1975.

U. S. Army. <u>Historical Preservation: Administrative Procedures, Technical Manual</u>. TM 5-801-1. Washington, DC: Headquarters, Dept. of the Army, 1975.

ADDITIONAL SOURCES

The Council on America's Military Past used to be named the Council on Abandoned Military Posts. Now based at P. O. Box 1151, Ft. Myer, VA 22211, CAMP publishes two useful publications in military history and historic preservation. Its newsletter, <u>Heliogram</u> focuses on current trends in preserving military history sites and its magazine, <u>Periodical</u>, publishes studies in military history.

The files of the National Register of Historic Places contain detailed information on specific structures such as the armories discussed in this essay. Its "inventory--nomination form" is a good starting place for research into any structure already on the National Register. The National Register, based in Washington, DC, is part of the Department of the Interior.

This essay originally appeared in the June 1977 <u>Push Pin Post</u>.

Your Summer Vacation Part I

The National Guard, as the oldest of the nation's military services, has left a well-commemorated record across the United States. Why not take in part of that heritage while on your vacation travels this summer? Possibilities for combining Guard history and vacation fun into two broad categories: historic places and museums.

The *National Register of Historic Places* (1976 ed.) lists approximately 296 different locations which start with the word "fort." While not all of these are military places, that number should give you an idea of the potential places to visit in just that one category. The *Register* lists some 12,000 properties first by state, then by county. It is available in large libraries for trip planning.

Museums of interest to Guardsmen and women are scattered throughout the country. There are two in Washington, D.C. that should be of particular interest to those visiting the capital city. First, of course, is the Heritage Gallery in the National Guard Memorial of the National Guard Association, One Massachusetts Ave., N.W., just one block west from the National Visitors Center in Union Station, and three blocks north from the Capitol. It's open weekdays. Their displays include an exhibit of model aircraft, tracing the history of military aviation and a one-of-a-kind set of wood carvings of the militia of every state. Also in Washington, The Smithsonian's Museum of History and Technology has an Armed Forces Hall. A special feature of the Hall for the entire family is the Discovery Corner devoted to the "Spirit of 1776," the everyday life of the citizen-soldier during the American Revolution. Demonstrations are held Tuesday through Saturday, 11 a.m.-2 p.m.

Specialized museums devoted to military history are located throughout the Eastern United States. In the South, to give one example, is the Citadel. This Military College of South Carolina in Charleston has a museum devoted to the history of the state forces known as the South Carolina Corps of Cadets.

The museum, located next to the library, includes models of forts, uniforms, and state streamers authorized to the Corps. Several states have museums devoted to their military heritage. The Pennsylvania Military Museum, Box 148, Boalsburg, Penn., 16827, displays several periods of conflict. The displays include a number of period uniforms, cannons and other firearms, seven cased dioramas, and an entire room depicting a World War I battlefield complete with a trench, Renault tank, 1918 GMC ambulance, and a 1916 Dodge truck. That museum is closed Mondays and major holidays.

Further west, the Kentucky Military History Museum, East Main Street—U. S. 60, Frankfort, Ky., 40601, open seven days a week, covers the military history of that state, including its participation in the National Guard, from the earliest days to the present.

This survey of historic places and museums is only a quick overview of some vacation time possibilities. A directory which lists these areas in detail is the *"Guide to U. S. Army Museums and Historic Sites"* (S/N 008-020-00561-4) which sells for $3 from the Government Printing Office, Washington, D.C., 20402. A little research before traveling will uncover other useful guides to supplement this outline. The National Park Service has published several topical books to assist tourists. For example, for those interested in Revolutionary War battlefields and structures, "Colonials and Patriots: Historic Places Commemorating our Forebears. 1700-1783" (1964) would be a useful aid. It is also available from the Government Printing Office.

Next month will be Part II: Possibilities west of the Mississippi.

—Martin K. Gordon

Photo courtesy Miss Gay M. Neufeld
Fort Frederica was built by General James Oglethorpe in 1736 for protection of English settlers in Georgia against Spanish advances. A center of militia activities in that era, the Fort is now part of the National Park System. It is located at St. Simons Island, 12 miles from Brunswick, Ga.

Heritage Gallery of the National Guard Memorial
A parade of custom molded and beautifully painted models of colonial militia marches to the beat of the drum and music of the fife in the Heritage Gallery.

YOUR SUMMER VACATION: PART I

The sources used are described in the essay. One of the sources is the brochures which various museums publish. The traveler interested in learning more about our military heritage through visiting these sites and museums should write ahead for brochures, current hours, and current exhibits.

This essay originally appeared in the May 1978 Push Pin Post.

YOUR SUMMER VACATION: PART II

Last month, this column examined three ideas through which you could incorporate the long heritage of the Guard into your summer vacation: researching places, visiting military museums, and visiting historic locations. This month's continuation discusses the same suggestions for travel west of the Mississippi River.

The National Park Service has published three books which can be obtained either through most libraries or by mail from the Government Printing Office, Washington, D.C. 20402. The order numbers are also provided. The books discuss places of interest to students of our military heritage.

The first book covers "early" sites throughout the country. "Explorers and Settlers: Historic Places Commemorating the Early Exploration and Settlement of the United States" (S/N 024-005-00006-2, $7.60). The second book studies the peaceful aspects of western development, "Prospector, Cowhand, and Sodbuster: Historic Places Associated with the Mining, Ranching, and Farming Frontiers in the Trans-Mississippi West" (S/N 024-005-00005-4, $5.90). The third volume uses specifically military themes and should be of the most interest. "Soldier and Brave: Historic Places Associated with Indian Affairs and the Indian Wars in the Trans-Mississippi West" (S/N 024-005-00236-7, $7.10).

A representative National Guard museum of the type that is evolving throughout the country is the 45th Infantry "Thunderbird" Division Museum located one-fourth mile east of Eastern Oklahoma City, Okla., at 2145 NE 36 Street. It is free and open 9-5 Tuesday through Friday and 1-5 Saturday and Sunday.

The history displayed and explained in the museum begins with the early Oklahoma Indian and territorial militias. Through a combination of topical and branch exhibits, the military history of the region is reflected through such displays as a World War I machine gun emplacement, a chapel display, an infantry room, an artillery room, and a recreation of part of Adolf Hitler's World War II apartment.

Oklahoma militiamen fought in the Spanish-American War, both World Wars, the Mexican Border action, and the Korean War when the 45th was one of the first two divisions to be called into active duty. Those activities, plus the peacetime call-ups for disaster relief operations and civil disturbance control operations, are all represented in the museum.

A different place of great interest is Fort Stevens State Park, nine miles west of Astoria, Ore., at the mouth of the Columbia River. Fort Stevens offers a combination of several hundred campsites, other recreational facilities, and over 100 years of Guard history.

The site was originally fortified with earthworks during the Civil War. But the Army, although it had engineers in the area, lacked the artillerymen necessary for manning the new harbor defenses it was building in 1863-64. One of the expedients that the commanders on the west coast used was to take the new 8th California Regiment of Infantry and, with the consent of California's Governor F. F. Low, turn its Companies A and B into artillerymen. Thus, Company B, 8th Infantry California Volunteers April 26, 1865, became the first unit stationed at Fort Stevens to operate its defenses. Captain Gaston d'Artois of the 8th has the distinction of being the first commanding officer of the fort.

The defenses at the mouth of the Columbia underwent many changes as artillery grew more powerful and the engineers responded with new and larger fortifications. Battery Russell, adjacent to the park area, is a good example of early 20th century coastal defenses at their peak. It was the last of the concrete emplacements built at Fort Stevens, being completed in 1904. It was armed with two 10-inch rifles on disappearing carriages. Guns of that type were designed to fire a projectile of 617 pounds, a distance of 16,290 yards, using a propellant powder charge of 182 pounds. This Battery and several others were used by the 249th Coast Artillery, Oregon National Guard, as training sites in the 1920s and 1930s.

On September 16, 1940, the 249th Coast Artillery was inducted into federal service at Salem, Ore., and stationed at the Harbor Defenses of the Columbia, which included Fort Stevens and its Battery Russell. Late on the night of June 21, 1942, still in the first year of World War II, a Japanese submarine surfaced off-shore and began to shell the Battery. The Guardsmen of the fort were eager to return the enemy fire. The harbor defense commander decided otherwise, because the submarine was out of range of his guns and he would only be revealing his positions by opening fire. The submarine failed to cause any significant damage. Nevertheless, Fort Stevens, defended by the Oregon National Guard, holds the historic distinction of being the first continental American military installation to come under foreign attack since the War of 1812, which ended 127 years before this action.

Information on Fort Stevens, including the availability of campsite reservations and the related fees, can be obtained by calling toll-free 800-452-5687 Monday through Friday.

After all, from the deserts of the southwest to the ocean beaches of the northwest, the Guard has been there.

—Martin K. Gordon

Fort Stevens State Park on the northern Oregon coast in Clatsop County today includes the historic remains of old Fort Stevens, a military installation established during the Civil War by the U.S. Army. Battery Russell, shown here, was the last concrete gun emplacement constructed. It was completed in 1904 and was deactivated in 1944. It was the last installation of its type within the continental U.S. to be active, and the only one which was fired upon by the enemy during World War II. This scene shows a large 10-inch rifle at Battery Russell being loaded (left) and fired during a practice exercise in the 1930s. All guns have been removed but Battery Russell has been partially restored by the State and is open to visitors.
Oregon Department of Transportation

YOUR SUMMER VACATION: PART II

BIBLIOGRAPHY

<u>OKLAHOMA</u>

<u>45th Division Museum: The Story of Oklahoma's Citizen-Soldier</u>. Brochure pub. by the 45th Division Museum, 2145 NE 36 Street, Oklahoma City, OK 73111.

<u>OREGON</u>

Hanft, Marshall. <u>The Cape Forts: Guardians of the Columbia</u>. Portland, OR: Oregon Historical Society, 1973.

    The standard history of coastal fortifications at the mouth of the Columbia River.

Oregon. State Highway Division. <u>Fort Stevens Historical Walking Tour</u>.

    A leaflet which contains information on each building at Fort Stevens.

U. S. Army. Center of Military History. Organizational History Branch. "Unit File: 249th Coast Artillery."

This essay originally appeared in the June 1978 <u>Push Pin Post</u>.

The Great Chicago Fire

More than one controversy was started along with the fire in Mrs. O'Leary's barn that fateful Sunday night of October 8, 1871, when the Great Chicago Fire started there. That fire lasted until early Tuesday morning October 10th. It burned out an area of 3.32 miles which included the entire central business district of the city. About 98,500 people were left homeless and there never has been a complete list of the estimated 300 persons killed in the fire. Also lost were 17,450 buildings and much of the city's industrial capacity, valued at between $196,000,000 and $200,000,000.

Monday, October 9th, while the fire was still raging, Major J.F. Alstrup volunteered his three companies of Scandinavian westsiders whose homes had not suffered much damage, for active duty to assist the police in maintaining order. The Police Superintendent immediately accepted their offer and thus the battalion designated Norwegian Guards, State Militia, became the first military force to arrive on the scene to assist the civil authorities. They remained on active duty for 15 days patrolling streets, and guarding railroad depots, relief committee storehouses and distributing headquarters. Each squad of three or four was placed under a regular policeman who traveled with and supervised them.

Acting upon the request of Mayor R.B. Mason, Governor John M. Palmer sent 315 additional militiamen into Chicago under the command of his adjutant general while the fire was still active. More companies were to follow. These organized militia companies included Captain Cyrus Donegan's black Springfield Zouave Liberty Guards, Captain H.D. Kuhlmann's Bloomington German National Guards, Professor E. Snyder's students composing the Champaign Cadets, and other units from around the state. Some units were sent home after the fire burned itself out. Others were to stay until the 24th as part of one of the most controversial impromptu militia units of 19th century America, the First Regiment Chicago Volunteers.

Along with the national confusion of the disaster, rumors were started about arsonists and looters active in the city. More rumors reported that bands of "toughs" were coming to Chicago to create more problems for the city. The Republican Mayor Mason, perhaps afraid that the Democratic Governor Palmer would not do enough to maintain order in Chicago, issued a most unusual proclamation on the 11th, the day after the fire ended. He wrote, "The preservation of the good order and peace of the city is hereby entrusted to Lieutenant General P.H. Sheridan, United States Army." Sheridan, the Civil War hero, was at that time commanding the Army's Department of the Missouri and was headquartered in Chicago. The police were ordered to cooperate with him. Thus, the Mayor, without contacting either the state or federal authorities in Washington, turned over all police powers in the city to an Army general. Sheridan immediately appointed a former Civil War general living in Chicago, Frank T. Sherman, to the rank of colonel of the First Regiment and ordered him to raise 19 companies of 90 men plus officers for 20 days special service in patrolling Chicago. He was to recruit among the 15,000 Civil War veterans then in the city.

Frank recruited a combination of State Militia companies then on active duty, citizens of Chicago, veterans or not, and, the students at the University of Chicago. Meanwhile, Governor Palmer, not knowing of this regiment, dismissed the State Militia from active service.

The Governor found out about the regiment after Private Theodore N. Treat, a University of Chicago student enlisted in the 20-day regiment, shot and fatally wounded Colonel Thomas W. Grosvenor, a disabled Civil War militiaman

Chicago Historical Society

This pencil sketch, "Who Goes There?" by artist Alfred R. Waud, depicts an episode in which the artist and the reporter working with him were stopped by a sentry on their way to the train station. The shooting of Colonel Grosvenor by a sentry was done in an undamaged part of Chicago.

and municipal attorney. Grosvenor had been walking home about midnight from a friend's house when the sentry stopped him. Grosvenor ignored the student's request for the password and started to continue home. The student shot him. A Cook County Coroner's investigation rejected Treat's defense that he had been merely obeying his military superiors who had told him to shoot anyone who did not give the proper password or countersign. He was accused of murder.

Needless to say, Governor Palmer viewed as illegal this militia regiment organized solely on the authority of a regular Army general acting with only a mayoral proclamation to support him. He asked the Illinois Attorney General to investigate whether or not Mayor Mason, General Sheridan, and Colonel Sherman should be charged for murder along with Private Treat on the grounds that their orders were illegal. Palmer argued that an Army general had no constitutional authority to come into a state and raise his own militia without even notifying the state's governor of his actions. The state legislature passed resolutions denouncing Sheridan's orders. Meanwhile, Mayor Mason asked Sheridan to request the Department of War to station four companies of regulars in Chicago in case looters tried to seize the relief supplies. He complied and that only upset the Governor still more. Palmer challenged President Ulysses S. Grant's authority to station regular troops in Chicago. The arguments went on. The case of Private Treat, the sentry, dropped from the discussions.

As the political debates over the constitutionality of Sheridan's actions continued, two points became clear about the role of the organized militia. First, they were on the scene before the frontier-oriented regular forces could race to Chicago. Secondly, the impact of the militia can be summed up in the words of the Adjutant-General of Illinois' report on the performance of his men, "Their presence evidently contributed to restore the confidence of the alarmed citizens, and rough as some of them (laborers, white and black, who had shouldered the musket in their working garb,) may have looked, their soldier-like dignified conduct must have impressed the citizens of Chicago, wherever they were stationed, that there was reliable help enough for them from their fellow-citizens of Illinois."

—Martin K. Gordon

THE GREE CHICAGO FIRE

BIBLIOGRAPHY

STATE DOCUMENTS

These documents were published without imprint information and are bound and cataloged in various ways in different libraries. They are all essential to an understanding of the role of the militia in the Chicago Fire. These documents are listed in chronological order.

Illinois. Adjutant General. *Adjutant-General's Report*. October 15, 1871. 5 pp.

A report to Governor John M. Palmer.

Illinois. Executive Department. *Letter to the Attorney-General*. October 28, 1871. 4 pp.

A request from the governor for an investigation of the actions of the military forces in Chicago after the Fire.

_____. *Messages From the Governor*. November 15, 1871. 23pp. and December 9, 1871. 16pp.

Reports to the state legislature on events in Chicago after the Fire.

Illinois. House of Representatives. Select Committee on the Governor's Messages of Nov. 15 & Dec. 9, 1871. *Report*. Springfield: Illinois State Journal Print., 1872.

This separately published document includes evidence, recommendations, and a minority report relating to the Fire.

Illinois. Adjutant General. *Report*. 1872, 1873-1874 biennial printing.

SECONDARY ACCOUNTS

Chicago Historical Society. *The Great Chicago Fire, October 8-10, 1871*. Chicago: Chicago Historical Society, n.d.

A fact sheet and bibliography.

Collins, Holdridge O. *History of the Illinois National Guard from the Organization of the First Regiment in September 1874, to the Enactment of the Military Code in May, 1879*. Chicago: Press of Black & Beach, 1884.

Culver, Virginia. "The Great Chicago Fire of 1871." *Coinage* 7 (November 1971): 66-67.

Discusses the work of the artist Alfred R. Waud after the Fire.

Almost all histories of the Chicago Fire and of Illinois politics for this time period shed light on this episode.

This essay originally appeared in the April 1978 *Push Pin Post*.

The Johnstown Flood

Days of unusually heavy rains bloated the Conemaugh River Reservoir beyond the capacity of the South Fork Dam. The dam burst on May 31, 1889, sending 78 million gallons of water sweeping westward through the valley that cradled the manufacturing city of Johnstown, Pennsylvania.

The city was quickly covered by thirty feet of swirling water. When the wave had passed, 2,200 people had died, and ten million dollars in property damage was left to those who remained in the valley.

If that incident happened today, the National Guard would be called out, and the Small Business Administration would move in to provide financial assistance. Even in 1889, the Guard was ready to move into Johnstown when they heard the news. Brigadier General Daniel Hartman Hastings, the state's Adjutant General, rushed to the city to offer help from the National Guard. Members of the Washington Infantry and Pittsburgh's Battery "B" were sent in by the Pittsburgh Chamber of Commerce.

This Library of Congress photo shows Guardsmen camped high above the devastated city

Johnstown city officials surprised the Guardsmen and General Hastings by refusing the offered assistance. The Guardsmen had already begun pulling bodies from the wreckage when they were sent home for acting without orders from the Governor.

Before they could pack up and leave the city, fires, and rumors of riots, fist fights, and looting swept the huddled survivors. Johnstown officials changed their minds and asked Governor James Beaver to send in the National Guard to help preserve order and to help in the rescue effort.

Pittsburgh's 14th Regiment and Johnstown's Company "H" were called in, bringing the total of Guardsmen to over 500. Most of the men remained on duty until late in June, and one company stayed in the city until the end of the summer.

The Guard's efforts during those months were similar to missions today. The Guardsmen helped with food, clothing, shelter, and medical supplies. They kept order after martial law was declared. They acted as coordinators for the assistance that poured in from federal and state agencies and from private citizens.

The services of the Guard in emergencies haven't changed significantly in the last hundred years. That's why the Guard is such a vital part of the local community today.

This young Guardsman knew he was posing for posterity. Photo courtesy of the Camera Shop, Johnstown, Pa.

Air to Air Refueling

Through increased cooperation between Active and Reserve forces, the Air National Guard has been taking on increased responsibility for a tactical operation that began as a barnstorming daredevil's routine.

In November, 1921, Wesley May was credited with the first air-to-air refueling. He crawled from wing to wing with a five gallon gas can strapped to his back.

From a barnstorming stunt, Army fliers began refining the idea for its tactical potential. Hoses and hand operated pumps were used in the first military refueling operations that were sufficiently developed to allow a flight endurance record of 150 hours in 1929. The six-day flight was made possible by 42 in-flight pit stops.

Progress slowed during World War II, but by the early '50's, a 500 gallon-per-minute pump gave the Strategic Air Command the technology to renew interest in midair refueling. Next, "wings" were put on the boom that had replaced the gas hose. The wings allowed pilots to control the position of the boom and greatly decreased the skills needed to accomplish refueling.

The SAC refinements made it possible for one tanker to refuel an entire formation. With proven effectiveness, other commands began to receive equipment and training for midair refueling.

The Tactical Air Command was the first to use the techniques in actual, tactical conditions. In-flight refueling was used to speed the deployment of TAC's Composite Air Strike Force to the Middle East in 1958 and again, just six weeks later, to the Formosan Straits.

More than nine years of constant use in the Southeast Asian conflict was the final proof of the value of midair refueling. The tankers and equipment are used by thirteen commands, including the Air National Guard. The Guard now has an on-going responsibility for some refueling operations.

Wesley May couldn't have seen all this as he crawled through the struts of a Lincoln Standard Biplane.

Courtesy TAC Press Service, Sgt. John Taska

THE JOHNSTOWN FLOOD

BIBLIOGRAPHY

Connelly, Frank, and Jenks, George C. Official History of the Johnstown Flood. Pittsburgh, Journalist Publishing Co., 1889.

    This source must be used with caution.

Federal Writers' Project, Pennsylvania. The Floods of Johnstown. Johnstown: Published by the Mayor's Committee of the City of Johnstown, PA., 1939.

McCullough, David G. The Johnstown Flood. New York: Simon and Schuster, 1968.

McLaurin, J. J. The Story of Johnstown: Its Early Settlement, Rise and Progress, Industrial Growth, and Appalling Flood on May 31st 1889. Harrisburg: James M. Place, Publisher, 1890.

    Chapter XXVI, "Under Military Authority," as a good account of the work of the military in the disaster relief operations.

Strayer, Harold D., and London, Irving L. A Photographic Story of Johnstown Flood: Most Complete Collection of 1889 Flood Pictures Ever Published. Johnstown: The Camera Shop. 1964.

This essay originally appeared in the April 1976 Push Pin Post.

"Yes, the Guard helped, but..."

Early in the morning of Wednesday 18 April 1906, one of the most memorable earthquakes in American history struck San Francisco. It started a large number of major fires in the city. When firemen were finally able to stop the fires three days later, approximately 500 city blocks or 4.7 square miles in the heart of the city had been destroyed. Both the National Guard and the Regular Army responded immediately—without waiting for formal orders. Brigadier General John A. Koster, commanding general of the Second Brigade, California National Guard, headquartered in San Francisco, was on a field trip with the state's Adjutant General Joseph B. Lauck. When General Koster returned, he found almost all of his Guardsmen already performing patrol duty.

Guard and Regular Army duties during that catastrophe could be divided into the categories of relief from suffering, the prevention of looting and the maintenance of order, and assisting in stopping the spread of the post-earthquake fires that were doing great damage to the city.

There was a lot of confusion at first as Guardsmen, Regulars, and citizen volunteers rushed to dispense aid without any controls. At first, scarce supplies of drinking water were given away as they were brought into the city without any effort to insure fair distribution. Food, particularly in some of the other cities to which residents had fled, was given out lavishly without any controls over quantity. Eventually the Guardsmen and the Regulars, cooperating informally through parallel chains of command, established systems to insure relief was given in fair quantities and only to the truly destitute. At one time, the Guard was feeding 25,000 to 30,000 persons daily.

The same day as the earthquake, Mayor Eugene E. Schmitz authorized "The Federal Troops, the members of the Regular Police Force and all Special Police Officers" to kill any looters or other criminals caught in the commission of their crimes. To help maintain order with a minimum of confusion, the city was at first districted into thirds, with the Guard, the Army, Navy and Marines, and the police each patrolling a district. During this time of state and federal assistance to the local authorities (martial law was never declared in San Francisco during this period) only nine deaths were due to violence. Two were attributed to the actions of California National Guardsmen acting in the line of duty. The two Guardsmen who were accused of the shootings were investigated by the judge advocate's department and found

The Bancroft Library

Guardsmen and others set sticks of dynamite to bring down dangerously tottering walls. Their seemingly random blastings during the fire did little to control the blaze and brought forth public criticism. If the explosive charges used were too large, the building would blow outwards and start new fires. Once again the problem was not the lack of enthusiasm but the lack of training on the part of the Guardsmen.

justified in their drastic actions. The Guardsmen were both subsequently tried in a civil court and freed after the trial.

Indeed, Major General Adolphus W. Greely, USA, commanding the Pacific Division of the Army, reporting fairly on this episode also hit upon one of the key concerns of the National Guard. General Greely wrote in his official report, "Some local feeling was aroused in the city against the Guard through the unfortunate fact that two San Franciscans... were shot by members of the Guard on April 19. The services of the Guard necessarily entailed hardships, through sacrifice of personal and material interests while on emergency duty. No doubt exists that the young men of the Guard were intelligent, well meaning, subordinate, and zealous. They were always judged by me from this standpoint, due consideration being given for their youthfulness and inexperience. This inexperience is alleged to have caused them to occasionally ignore municipal authority."

Mayor Schmitz was not happy that the governor had allowed his National Guard to work in San Francisco without a formal request from local authorities. Schmitz was afraid, for political reasons, of a state force operating in his city that was not under his control. The mayor asked that the Guard be removed at the same time as General Greely was asking for 2,500 additional Regulars for the city. President Theodore Roosevelt overruled the request for the Regulars unless the Governor, George C. Pardee, a former member of the Guard, certified the need for the Regulars in order to maintain order in the city. The Governor refused to remove his Guardsmen and refused to admit that more Regulars were needed. Finally, General Greely convinced the Governor that the Regulars were needed strictly for relief work and Pardee then asked Roosevelt to authorize their use in San Francisco. Meanwhile, Governor Pardee received long petitions from local citizens praising the work of the state forces.

Eventually, as municipal police, fire, and sanitation forces returned to operating capacity both the state and federal forces were withdrawn. In spite of the shootings by young Guardsmen, in spite of the Mayor's fear that Governor Pardee would use the troops against him in political ways, the citizen-soldiers had performed well once again. As one petition, signed by over 20,000 residents put it, the services of the state forces, "have been of the very greatest value."

—Martin K. Gordon

"YES, THE GUARD HELPED, BUT..."

BIBLIOGRAPHY

Hudson, James J. "The California National Guard in the San Francisco Earthquake and Fire of 1906." *California Historical Quarterly* 55 (Summer 1976): 137-149.

Strobridge, William F. "Troops to the Rescue in San Francisco, 1906: Civil-Military Relations in the West." Paper presented at the Western History Association Conference, Denver, 1976.

U. S. Army. Pacific Division. *Earthquake in California April 18, 1906. Special Report of Maj. Gen. Adolphus W. Greely, U.S.A.* Washington: Government Printing Office, 1906.

The author acknowledges with gratitude the assistance of Colonel William F. Strobridge, USA (Ret.) with this essay.

This essay originally appeared in the December 1977 *Push Pin Post*.

The Hatfields, The McCoys, and the Citizen-Soldiers Get Involved in a Famous Feud

The Committee on the Militia of the House of Representatives in 1892 published another in Congress' ongoing studies of the American National Guard. The study included reports of the states' Adjutant-Generals on all active service periods of their respective forces from the end of the Civil War to the time of the report. Kentucky, the home of the great nineteenth century feud between the Hatfields and the McCoys, failed to submit information in that category. But the West Virginia report included this entry for January, 1888, "To suppress lawlessness and protect citizens from threatened violence growing out of Hatfield and McCoy feud," two companies totaling 77 men were called up but not actually deployed.

THE FEUD

That bland statement was the only mention of the famous country feud which nearly resulted in a fight between the states of Kentucky and West Virginia. Controversy exists over which incidents gave rise to the feud, which might even have started in Civil War days when William Anderson ("Devil Anse") Hatfield was an officer in the Confederate militia while the McCoys fought for the Union. A more immediate cause was the 1873 accusation of Randolph McCoy that Floyd Hatfield stole a pig that belonged to the McCoys. The resulting trial, to which both sides came heavily armed, proved nothing. Later, it was commonly believed that two McCoys had killed a Hatfield; but when the Hatfields brought the murderer to trial, he was acquitted with a verdict of justified killing in self-defense. Other incidents, such as a forbidden love affair between Johnson ("Johnse") Hatfield and Rose Anne McCoy, further fueled the feud. Stabbings, murder, and arson all fanned the flames of Hatfield-McCoy enmity.

THE FIGHT

The Hatfields lived in the West Virginia hills, and the McCoys just across the river in Kentucky. Over the years the states became embroiled in the feud between clans. December, 1887, a Kentucky posse crossed the state line and arrested Selkirk McCoy who had gone over to the Hatfields. (He was eventually charged with murder.) The West Virginia Hatfields were continually reminding their governor, E. Willis ("Windy") Wilson, that they could never receive a fair trial in Kentucky, that they were innocent anyway, and in any case,

"Devil Anse" Hatfield seated in the center of a group of Hatfields and other clansmen. Note that every man in this group is holding either a rifle or a pistol. (Photo courtesy of the Library of Congress)

the McCoys had never been punished for felonies they had committed in West Virginia. Under Hatfield leadership the West Virginians of Logan County carried out home guard duties as the Logan County Regulators, in case of a raid by Kentuckians allegedly enforcing the law.

January 19, 1888, in the Battle of Grapevine Creek, a Kentucky posse searching in West Virginia met a West Virginia posse looking for some Kentucky murderers. In the ensuing fight, one man was killed and one wounded. As Kentucky posses continued to raid into West Virginia, the state of West Virginia reacted at first by offering a reward for the Kentucky deputy sheriff and all 22 members of his posse.

THE MILITIA

Groups from both states soon began asking their governors for either arms for self-defense or state soldiers to defend them. Governor Simon Bolivar Buckner of Kentucky advised the petitioners to organize a local militia company under responsible leadership. He felt that a community should try to assist itself before calling for state assistance. In contrast, Governor Wilson of West Virginia replied to his petitioners by ordering two companies of militia to Charlestown, West Virginia. Buckner sent his adjutant general to the feud area to confer with Wilson's representative in an effort to avoid open warfare. Although Buckner had turned down petitions for the militia, he had alerted units for active duty.

Meanwhile, the Kentucky General Assembly was debating a bill authorizing six more troops for the state guard. A proposal that one of the new units should be located in the feud region caused the bill's defeat. During the discussion, legislators expressed their views by offering amendments specifying that the bill should not be interpreted as a declaration of war by Kentucky, and that instead of guns, "six good school teachers and two evangelists" should be sent to the turbulent counties.

At the scene of the troubles, the citizens of Logan Country, West Virginia, asked both governors to send the militia to the state borders. Sixty citizen-soldiers of the Goff and Auburn Guards of Ritchie County, first to volunteer their services, were called up for this peacekeeping duty. Other companies around the state also volunteered for active duty, but at this point Wilson learned that the clans had ceased their violent reprisals and that the border was calm. After more arguments, Governor Wilson took his fight with Kentucky to the courts, and marshals took over guarding the nine prisoners Kentucky had seized in West Virginia. The militias of the two states were never deployed against each other, and in time the legal processes reigned supreme. That ended the role of the militia in the feud of the Hatfields and the McCoys.

—Martin K. Gordon

THE HATFIELDS, THE McCOYS, AND THE CITIZEN-SOLDIERS

GET INVOLVED IN A FAMOUS FEUD

BIBLIOGRAPHY

Hatfield, Lawrence D. The True Story of the Hatfield-McCoy Feud. Charleston, WV: Jarrett Printing Company, 1944.

Jones, Virgil C. The Hatfields and the McCoys. Chapel Hill: Univ. of North Carolina Press, 1948.

Thomas, Jean. Big Sandy. New York: Henry Holt & Co., 1940.

U. S. Congress. House of Representatives. Committee on the Militia. Efficiency of the Militia. H. R. Rept. 754, 52d Cong., 1st sess., 1892.

This essay originally appeared in the June 1979 Push Pin Post.

What Do You Do When the Guard is Away?
Read On Dear Reader...

What does a state use for a military force when the National Guard is federalized? That question has come up a number of times in the recent past. It is considered important that each state have a military force under the control of the governor even during wartime so a state militia or state guard is usually organized during times of stress.

World War II prompted just such state action, and California was no exception to those states concerned with the need for a readily available local guard force. Between September 16, 1940, when President Franklin D. Roosevelt ordered the 250 and 251st Coast Artillery into federal service and April 1, 1941, when the Headquarters and Headquarters Battery of the 76th Field Artillery Brigade went into federal service, the entire California National Guard was federalized. But, many citizens had already begun to worry about the defense of the state and maintenance of order within its boundaries even before the first state unit was federalized. On August 18, 1940, the Southern California Home Defense Force was organized. Similar volunteer units sprang up elsewhere in the state and, indeed, around the country.

The creation of the State Guard was consistent with the American tradition of a local defense force based on the unorganized part of the militia. The State Guards were not given a dual status as possessed by the National Guard, but they were given dual missions. They could not be called into the federal service but their members were not exempt from the draft.

Section of Hq. Det. and Q. M. Det. Women's Branch, California State Guard.

They were expected, however, to join with the Federal Army in resisting invasion and sabotage and in assisting local police forces in maintaining domestic order. Their mission included resisting bombing raids, commando assaults, enemy paratrooper or hostile fifth column activities. In those bleak days after Pearl Harbor, any of those possibilities seemed possible. Some State Guard units even trained especially for guerrilla operations behind enemy lines. As Under Secretary of War Robert Patterson had warned in November 1940, "the wars of today know no front lines; a tiny village hundreds of miles from the theoretical front may suddenly become the scene of desperate and blazing action."

Against that background, the usual disagreements arose. There was an argument over the clause in the United States Constitution which forbids the states from keeping troops or ships of war in peacetime without permission of Congress. Congress solved this problem in 1940 when it authorized states to maintain state forces but only when all or part of that state's National Guard had been federalized, and only if the state's forces operated under regulations laid down by the Secretary of War for discipline and training. There were also arguments over who should pay the costs of the State Guards when on active duty. Congress finally decided that these costs were a state responsibility, but the California State Guard once had to wait seven weeks for its pay before the state legislature finally acknowledged the obligation.

The attack on Pearl Harbor caused the activation of the entire State Guard who then were rushed to guard such key areas as bridges, oilfields, military hospitals, power plants, radio stations, and water supplies from possible attacks. That Guard had, in October 1941, shortly before the start of the war, an authorized strength of 15,796 and an actual strength of 11,630 men. In the spring and summer of 1943, the State Guard, which by then included women, began to stand down from its guard duties. After the victory at

Long Beach Harbor Area
One of the most important posts in the harbor area. Just inside fenced-in enclosure are the main shut-off valves controlling oil flow of wells in background.

Guadalcanal, the state legislature faced with continual frustrations in trying to obtain draft exemptions for State Guardsmen as well as the high cost of maintaining the Guard, ordered Governor Earl Warren to return the bulk of the Guard to an inactive status. But the California State Guard continued to be of use in activities such as fighting forest fires until the California National Guard returned home after the end of the war.

Story by Martin Gordon

Golden Gate Bridge (Old Fort at Base of Bridge)
State Guardsman scans water for floating mines that may be cast adrift and that could enter bay area, endangering naval craft at anchor.

WHAT DO YOU DO WHEN THE GUARD IS AWAY?

BIBLIOGRAPHY

California. Adjutant General's Office. <u>California State Guard: A Manual for Period Instruction, Basic Subjects Only</u>. Sacramento: California State Printing Office, 1944.

_____. <u>History of the California State Guard</u>. Sacramento: California State Printing Office, 1946.

This essay originally appeared in the August 1976 <u>Push Pin Post</u>.

New Technology
Nineteenth Century Style

The Bicycle as a Military Weapon

The first suggestion that the velocipede or bicycle might be used as a new technological breakthrough for the infantry was published by a former United States Volunteer, General W. H. Brown in 1868. By the 1890s, both the regulars and the organized militia, then in the process of becoming the modern National Guard, began experimenting with the new machines. Those experiments, like many of more recent years, had the full backing of the industry which manufactured the potential war device. Manuals for the use of the bicycle in both the Army and the National Guard were written by well-known officers and then published by the Pope Manufacturing Company of Boston and Hartford, a bicycle-manufacturing firm. When the manuals were published commercially, the Pope Company placed full page ads in the manuals touting its products in such military-sounding phrases as "victory proclaims the vast superiority of Columbia Chainless Bicycles." Alongside such combinations of service and promotion, there was a genuine military interest in the bicycle in this country as well as in Europe and Japan.

These are two of the suggested formation positions, squad dismounted and inspection cycles, from Captain Giddings' *Manual for Cyclists*.

By the middle 1890s states such as Connecticut, New York, and West Virginia had bicycle units within the organized militia. While the regular Army experimented with a Bicycle Corps for long-distance maneuvering, the Guard considered using the bicycle soldiers as couriers, mounted infantry, a mobile defensive reserve, riot control units, and even in an ambulance capacity using two bicycles specially built to carry a stretcher mounted between them.

Both services agreed that the bicyclist was first a specialist in some arm or branch such an infantry or signaling and only secondarily a pedaler. With the exception of the weight limit, which was ten pounds lighter in the regular Army bicycle units, everyone would probably have agreed with the military bicycling principles of Captain Howard Giddings: "cyclists are

soldiers mounted on bicycles, either temporarily or permanently. They may be taken from any arm or branch of the service. Only young men of superior intelligence, temperate habits, and sound constitution, who have had not less than three years' experience in cycling, should be selected for this service. As a rule, they should not exceed 5 feet 8 inches in height nor 150 pounds in weight." Captain Giddings was a Connecticut Guardsman and author of the *Manual For Cyclists*, not a best seller, but a book of instructions on the military uses of the bicycle.

NEW TECHNOLOGY NINETEENTH CENTURY STYLE:
THE BICYCLE AS A MILITARY WEAPON

BIBLIOGRAPHY

Caidin, Martin, and Barbree, Jay. <u>Bicycles in War</u>. New York: Hawthorn Books, Inc., 1974.

Fletcher, Marvin E. "The Black Bicycle Corps." <u>Arizona and the West</u> (Autumn 1974): 219-232.

Giddings, Howard A., Capt. <u>Manual for Cyclists: For the Use of the Regular Army, Organized Militia, and Volunteer Troops of the United States</u>. Kansas City, MO: Hudson-Kimberly Pub. Co., 1898.

Ordway, Albert, Brig. Gen. <u>Cycle-Infantry Drill Regulations</u>. Boston: Pope Manufacturing Co., 1892.

    Includes a speech by Major General Nelson A. Miles, 31 May 1892, on "Military Cycling."

Riling, Ray. "Cycle Infantry Drill Regulations." <u>Military Collector & Historian</u> 13 (Spring 1961): 24-26.

This essay originally appeared in the May 1976 <u>Push Pin Post</u>.

Martin K. Gordon. (Army Times photograph by Kate Patterson)

The author is a professional military historian and writer on military subjects. Mr. Gordon holds the doctorate in American Civilization from The George Washington University and has also graduated from the Universities of Notre Dame and Wisconsin. His articles on the American militia are cited in the bibliographies published in this history. Additionally, he has written on the relationship of the military to the larger American culture and has lectured regularly on military history at the Smithsonian Institution in Washington, D.C. He is an active member of the American Military Institute, the Company of Military Historians, the Council on America's Military Past, and the United States Commission on Military History. He is currently employed with the Historical Division, U.S. Army Corps of Engineers and has worked for the History and Museums Division, Headquarters, U.S. Marine Corps.

Paris, France. American troops of the 28th Infantry Division march down the Champs Elysees in the "Victory parade," 1945. (Photo by Poinsett)

Interesting Facts About America's Citizen Soldiers
DID YOU KNOW . . .

- The Organized Militia has been in existence since 1636.
- Marksmanship was a problem at the battles of Lexington and Concord.
- George Washington used experienced mariners called up for active duty in the militia to row him across the Delaware for his surprise assault on the British.
- The term "National Guard" began to replace the word "militia" in August 1824 as a result of a visit by Lafayette to the United States.
- The baggy trousers of the Civil War era Zouaves had a practical purpose.
- Air Guardsmen in many states had to provide their own airplanes before World War I.
- Blacks, Germans, Hispanics, Poles, Jews, Irish, and other ehtnic groups have participated in the heritage of the National Guard.
- Personalities as diverse as Edgar Allen Poe and Charles A. Lindbergh served in the Guard.
- National Guard units served in the defense of Bataan and Corregidor in the early battles of World War II.
- The physical heritage of the Guard is represented in museums and historic sites throughout the United States.

Imprint on the Nation is an excellent account of these and other highlights of the history of the National Guard. Martin K. Gordon's book is not just for military personnel or the military history buff but is for anyone who enjoys a good story. His essays reflect the contributions and traditions of the United States' oldest military organizations, the participation of citizen soldiers in disaster rescue operations, wars, riots, and the impact of those soldiers on such aspects of American culture as its museums, sermons, and music.

"In all of the attention which has been paid to U.S. military history is has often struck me as ironic that there is such a dearth of literature on the oldest of our nation's military institutions, the National Guard.

"This collection of essays by Martin K. Gordon promises to go a long way toward the correction of the deficiency noted above. This collection is a vivid demonstration of the widespread and yet localized character of the Guard. In its panoply of parades, its great urban armories, its responses to disaster, its historic places and its colorful people, Gordon has succeeded in showing something of the face of the soldiers of the States and their long tradition of setting aside civilian world responsibilities to particpate in the nation's wars and battles."

— From the Foreword by BRUCE JACOBS
Major General, Army National Guard
Publisher, *National Guard* Magazine